Planning Perfect

PARTIES

The *Girls' Guide* to
Fun, Fresh, Unforgettable *Ever*

by Jen Jones

TABLE OF CONTENTS

PART ONE:
Planning Nitty-Gritty

Getting Started **5**

Get in Check **6**

Save the Date **8**

Party Pals **10**

Do the Math **12**

The 'Rents: How to Deal **14**

You're Invited **16**

Shop 'Til You Drop **18**

Kitchen Confidential **20**

So Cheesy **22**

Amazeballs **24**

Signature Sips **26**

Your Party Style **28**

Let The Games Begin! **30**

Clean Sweep **32**

Countdown to Fun **34**

One-Stop Sweet Shoppe **36**

Party Pom-Poms **38**

PART TWO:
Party Inspiration & Ideas

The Big Idea **41**

Party Like A Rock Star **42**

Tea Time **44**

Pamper Me Pretty **46**

A Pirate P-arrrrrty **48**

Movie Under the Stars **50**

You've Got Game **52**

'Stache Bash **54**

Party Gras **56**

Shine On **58**

Crazy Carnival **60**

Theme-o-Rama **62**

PART THREE:
C-I-Y Chica

Make and Take **67**
Hitting the Right Note **68**
Insta-Atmosphere: Quick Tricks **70**
Tiny Treats: Favors That Rock **72**
Nifty Nails **74**
Hot Rods **76**
Crepe Expectations **78**
Karaoke Queens **80**
T.G.G. Totally Gorgeous
    Guestbook **82**
Smart Cookie **84**
Good Clean Fun **86**
Lay It On **88**
Light-Up Lantern **90**
Outlook: Good **92**
Teeny Umbrellas, Big Fun! **94**
Better With Ranch **96**
Feeling Festive **98**

PART FOUR:
Party Time!

P-A-R-T-Y! **101**
Par-tay! (It's Finally Time) **102**
De-Stress R/x **104**
Get the Party Started **106**
The Usual Suspects **108**
Hostess with the Mostest:
    Do's & Don'ts **110**
Dealing with Disaster!
    Party Crises 411 **112**
Keep the Party Poppin' **114**
Putting the "Super"
    in Supervision **116**
It's Over! Now What? **118**
Gracias, Merci, Thank You! **120**
Picture Perfect **124**
The Fun Never Ends **126**

4

Getting Started

It's not hard to see why people love parties so much. After all, they're festive, fun, and celebrate something that's really important—friendship. The best hostesses throw parties that bring new people together. That's where you come in!

The trick is planning a party that your friends won't forget. Creativity is the key—any interest or hobby can be transformed into a party theme. Get inspired with 10 unforgettable party themes. Then find oodles of ideas for making your party pop!

Of course, it's true that a hostess' work is never done. Endless to-do lists and hands-on tasks often translate to hard work for a party planner. Luckily, it can also be a lot of fun—and a lot easier with insider intel! The right info can keep you organized, savvy, and sane as you plan your big shindig. Learn ways to cover all of the bases while preparing for your party—and hit a home run with the result.

Get in Check

Use this page as a one-stop shop for all things party prep! This general checklist covers all of the to-do's that need to happen before your big day.

4 to 6 Weeks Ahead

- [ ] get your parents' permission
- [ ] finalize details—date, time, theme, location, etc.
- [ ] research costs and set a budget
- [ ] make your guest list
- [ ] rent any needed equipment (such as a karaoke machine)
- [ ] start getting jazzed for your party!

3 Weeks Ahead

- [ ] assemble and send out invites
- [ ] start planning the menu and signature sips
- [ ] make a list of necessary supplies and décor

2 Weeks Ahead

- [ ] figure out the fun stuff—games, music, favors
- [ ] shop for non-perishable items like favors and décor

1 Week Ahead

- [ ] collect all R.S.V.P.s and finalize guest count
- [ ] assemble any gift bags/décor
- [ ] make your party playlists

1 to 3 Days Ahead

- [ ] buy food and drink items, as well as any other necessities not already purchased
- [ ] prepare as much food as possible and store in the refrigerator or freezer
- [ ] clean the house and/or backyard

 Get your own downloadable checklist at
www.perfectpartiesguide.com/downloads/checklist

Save the Date

Soccer practice and dance class and family parties, oh my! With lots of busy schedules to work around (including your own), planning a party often requires a good strategy and a solid plan. Here are some tips to help out with timing:

- Avoid holding your party too close to major holidays. Many of your friends might not be around on Easter weekend or Thanksgiving. Check the calendar for popular vacation days too, such as Memorial Day or spring break. If you do choose to host a holiday party, make peace with the fact that a few peeps might have to miss out.

- Put your head together with the rest of your family and make sure that there are no scheduling conflicts. If you have a few besties that you can't be without, run the date by them as well.

- Don't forget about Mother Nature! Be sure to have a backup location if you're planning an outdoor party.

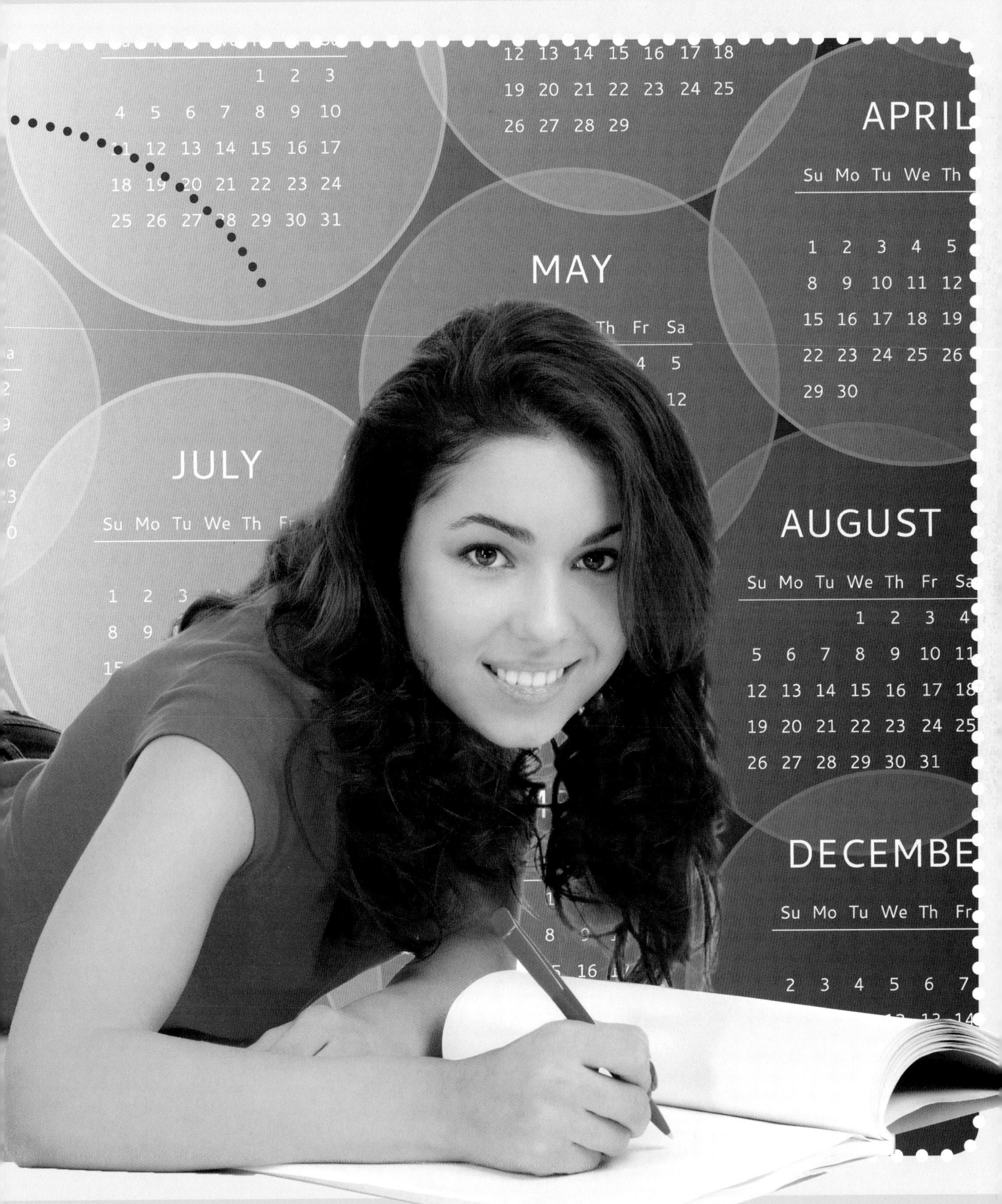
APRIL
MAY
JULY
AUGUST

Party Pals

Curious what "R.S.V.P." stands for? Wonder no more. It stems from the French phrase *Répondez, s'il vous plait.* In other words, "Please reply!"

R.S.V.P.s are great tools for hostesses. Most event planning experts say to expect anywhere from one-half to two-thirds of your invited guests to show up. Even with that stat, it's nice to have a concrete number! Requesting an R.S.V.P. provides just that by helping you keep track of who is—and isn't—able to make it to your party.

When sending invites, be sure to include a deadline to respond. The deadline date should be at least one week before the party date. If you don't hear back from everyone in time, just make a casual phone call or e-mail to follow up. Once you have a final list, you'll know who your party peeps are!

Ask Mizz Manners

Q. DO I HAVE TO INVITE EVERYONE IN MY CLASS?

A. Always a tricky question! It's a nice gesture to invite as many people as possible. But sometimes budget, location, or other factors just won't allow it. The best thing to do in this situation is to avoid hurt feelings.

Avoid passing out invites at school. Instead, e-mail or send invites directly to your friends' homes. If anyone asks why he or she wasn't invited, just be honest. Simply say that this time you're keeping it small, but you'd love to host a bigger bash in the future! (More excuses for parties? Yes, please.)

Do the Math

Before you can start planning, setting a budget is a must! Start by setting an overall spending limit. Talk with your parents about what they are willing to contribute to the party. Add that to the amount you've planned to spend. (For example, if you're contributing $50 and your parents are giving $200, you've got $250 to work with.) Divide that total by the number of people expected to attend. That's how much you can spend per person.

Next, figure out what's most important to you. Is it décor? Entertainment? Food and beverages? Making a list of priorities will help you see how to divide the funds. As you shop, keep a running expense total so that you don't blow the budget!

The Look for Less

Don't stress if you're not on a Beverly Hills budget. It's more than possible to throw a memorable party that feels–and looks–like a million bucks. Believe it or not, the dollar store can be a source of lots of super-cute, useful finds. Look there for anything from colorful drinking glasses to art supplies. It's a fun place to go on a supermarket sweep!

Quick Swaps For Saving Moolah

snail mail invites)))➤ e-mail
super-sized guest list)))➤ smaller guest list
full menu)))➤ apps and desserts
paper plates and cups)))➤ plates and cups your family owns

PARTY BUDGET

Party Budget Total: _____

Item	% of Budget	$ Allowance	$ Parents
FOOD	50%		
DECORATIONS	25%		
INVITATIONS	10%		
TABLEWARE	5%		
FAVORS	5%		
MISC.	5%		

 Use our online budgeting tool at
www.perfectpartiesguide.com/budget-tool

The 'Rents: How to Deal

You've picked your theme and set a date. But just because you got the go-ahead from your parents doesn't mean you're now off the hook! Involving the adults in your life is a must for getting things done. It's important to make sure everyone is on the same page. About a month before the big day, sit down to discuss essentials and expectations.

Remember that your parents are giving their time and money to help you out. Let them help with the fun parts of the planning process. Respect their wishes before and during the party. If you're able to help pay for any part of the celebration, they'd probably love that too.

Things to go over:

- [ ] party budget
- [ ] number of guests
- [ ] activities
- [ ] details such as décor, food, and drinks
- [ ] shopping schedule
- [ ] ground rules
- [ ] supervision
- [ ] any concerns that could affect the party

For more planning and budgeting tips,
www.perfectpartiesguide.com/tips

You're Invited

The two words everyone loves to hear—You're invited! Invites are an awesome way to get people excited for your party. They also set the tone for what's to come.

You've Got Mail

There are two main ways to send invites—e-mail and snail mail. Both have benefits. E-mail is a quick, easy budget trimmer. Snail mail makes guests feel special and often allows for more creativity. The good news? There's no wrong way to do it! If you decide to go the e-mail route, check out invitation websites for fun and fab design options.

One tip—if you send invites over the Internet, check your privacy settings! Make sure guests can't share or forward their invites, or you might end up with lots of extra attendees.

Don't-Miss Details

Wondering what info to include? Use this handy-dandy rundown:

- your name
- party occasion or theme
- brief description of the party
- day, date, and time
- location and address
- suggested dress code (if necessary)
- R.S.V.P. date and contact info

Get customizable invites at
www.perfectpartiesguide.com/invites

'80s PARTY

Mackenzie's '80s-Tastic Birthday Bash!
Hosted By Mackenzie Martin

Girls just wanna have fun! Bust out your best neon and big hair!
Let's travel back in time together to the totally awesome '80s.

When:
Saturday, August 2nd
1:00 p.m. – 4:00 p.m.

Where:
Mackenzie's Time Machine
123 Main Street

Please R.S.V.P. no later than July 27th by e-mailing
mackenzie@emailvites.com or calling 555-xxx-xxxx.

Shop 'Til You Drop

Parties are like snowflakes in that no two are alike. However, there are certain staples that almost every hostess needs to throw a successful one. Use this sample shopping list to see what you might need. Off to the store you go!

Shopping List

- [ ] paper cups/plates
- [ ] plastic utensils
- [ ] napkins
- [ ] paper towels
- [ ] trash bags
- [ ] 1 pound (455 grams) of ice per person attending. (Plan for twice as much if the party is outdoors.)
- [ ] cleaning supplies
- [ ] tablecloth(s)
- [ ] candles (if celebrating a birthday)
- [ ] thank you notes

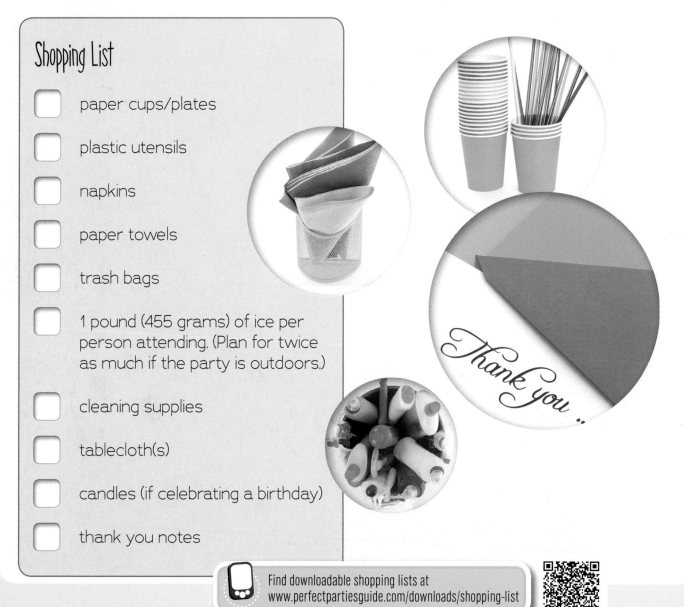

Find downloadable shopping lists at www.perfectpartiesguide.com/downloads/shopping-list

Your food and décor will depend on the menu and other details you decide on. For maximum organization, create a spreadsheet. Make a column for each category.

Fill it with shopping lists for each item. Highlight anything you already have at your house, such as markers and posterboard.

Spa Party Shopping List

Food	Drink	Décor
Polish Puffs: 3 cans colored frosting 2 bags marshmallows 1 bag chocolate chews	**All That Razz:** 2 packs fresh raspberries 4 lemons sparkling water	**Spa Welcome Sign:** posterboard stencil glitter pen markers

Smart Shopper

Want to avoid that "ouch" moment at the cash register? Shop smart! Check to see what you have around the house before your shopping trip. Compare prices online so you have an idea of price range. Dollar stores or thrift stores are also good places to find affordable party goods.

Coupon clipping can help save some dough. Check out the store's website for printable coupons before heading out to shop. When shopping online, look up coupon codes before you check out. Codes for discounts or free shipping are always nice finds.

Kitchen Confidential

Not quite a domestic diva just yet? Not to worry! No one expects you to transform overnight. Easy recipes can be just as tasty as expert ones. Here's what you need to know to conquer the kitchen with ease:

Organize and clean out the fridge to make room for all the new groceries. Pitch anything that's past its prime.

Try to choose recipes that use some of the same ingredients. It will simplify both shopping and cooking.

If possible, do a "dry run" of any new recipes before the party. Knowing how the recipes work (and taste) will come in handy. You'll also gain more kitchen confidence for the big day.

Know how you'll keep foods at their proper temp during the party. Hot foods should be kept at least 140 degrees Fahrenheit (60 degrees Celsius). Keep hot food safe by using chafing dishes, slow cookers, or warming trays. Cold foods should be kept at 40°F (4°C) or below. Keep things cool by using ice-filled nesting dishes.

So Cheesy

Now that you've conquered the kitchen, it's time to get cooking! Start with these simple cheese straws.  Then tackle the rest of the recipes until you're a master chef.

- ½ cup (120 milliliters) grated Parmesan cheese
- cutting board
- 1 package puff pastry
- 2 teaspoons (10 mL) Italian seasoning
- rolling pin
- pizza cutter
- baking sheet

1. Pre-heat the oven to 375°F (190°C).

2. Sprinkle half the Parmesan cheese across the cutting board. Lay a puff pastry sheet over the cheese-sprinkled board.

3. Scatter Italian seasoning and the rest of the cheese over the top of the pastry sheet.

4. Use a rolling pin to roll the dough until it is around ⅛-inch (.3-centimeter) thick. Press lightly, to make sure the cheese sticks to the dough.

5. Use a pizza cutter to cut the dough into long strips. Twist each strip several times and place on a greased baking sheet. Bake the cheese strips until they turn crispy and golden.

Finding Your Flavor

These easy, cheesy sticks are totally customizable! Find your favorite flavor by trying some of these recipe ideas.

- Use another type of cheese, such as Swiss, Cheddar, or Gouda, instead of Parmesan.

- Use dried chives, parsley, rosemary, oregano, sage, or thyme instead of Italian seasoning. Or try taco seasoning, curry powder, or cheese flavoring.

- Add sundried tomatoes, diced pepperoni or salami, or fresh minced garlic.

- Add sesame or poppy seeds, cayenne pepper, sea salt, or garlic powder.

- Try sweet instead of savory. Sprinkle twists with cinnamon sugar, cocoa powder, or brown sugar and candied nuts.

 Download this recipe, and others, at www.perfectpartiesguide.com/recipes

Amazeballs

Impress your friends with this quick, easy, and delicious cookie buttery treat!

- two bananas, mashed
- 1 cup (240 mL) quick oats
- ¼ cup (60 mL) chocolate candies
- 2 tablespoons (30 mL) cookie butter (also called speculoos or biscoff spread)

- 1 teaspoon (5 mL) vanilla extract
- nonstick baking sheet
- 1 cup (240 mL) white chocolate chips

1. Preheat the oven to 350°F (180°C).

3. Mix bananas, oats, candies, cookie butter, and vanilla together.

3. Take a spoonful of the mixture and roll it into a ball. Place the balls a few inches apart on a nonstick baking sheet.

4. Bake the cookies inside the oven for 15 minutes. Remove hot tray with oven mitts.

5. Drizzle melted white chocolate over cooled cookies.

Ask Mizz Manners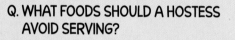

Q. WHAT FOODS SHOULD A HOSTESS AVOID SERVING?

A. Different experts will give different answers, but certain foods are widely thought to be party "don'ts." If you can, steer clear of messy finger foods like Buffalo wings and cheesy chips. They may be finger-lickin' good, but sticky or orange fingers are no fun. Also avoid stinky cheeses, fish dishes, anything garlicky, and hard-boiled eggs. Your nose will thank you.

Q. HELP! HOW MUCH FOOD IS TOO MUCH?

A. When it comes to party planning, always round up! Expect people to eat more than you think. Anticipate more guests arriving than you planned for. It's better to have too much than too little. Also, try to figure out which items might be the most popular. Bulk up on the foods that have a higher chance of being scarfed first.

If you can't buy any more of a main dish, have snacks such as fruit, veggies, or chips on hand. Snacks will help your guests fill up without stressing out your wallet.

Q. I'M ON A BUDGET. HOW CAN I FEED MY GUESTS ON A LIMITED AMOUNT OF MOOLAH?

A. Just because cash is tight doesn't mean you can't host a delicious get-together. Keep things low-key by holding a movie night with a popcorn bar. Host a tea party and serve just appetizers or desserts. Quiches, pasta salads, and chilis are easy, cost-effective, and can serve a crowd. For something more rustic, get outdoors! Roast hot dogs, baked potatoes, and marshmallows. There are tons of meal ideas for the hostess with limited funds!

More questions for Mizz Manners? Ask them at
MizzManners.perfectpartiesguide.com

25

Signature Sips

Ask yourself this question: "If my party were a beverage, what would it be?" The answer just might be your signature sip! Create a beverage that goes perfectly with your party's theme or color scheme. A signature sip at an Oscar viewing party might be "Red Carpet Punch." It's all about creativity! And speaking of creativity, there are plenty of ways to dress up your party drinks.

Rock the rim.

Rimming your beverage glass adds a whole new level of good taste. Wet the rim of the glass using water, a slice of fruit (such as a lemon, lime, or orange), or chocolate syrup. Gently dip the rim into a shallow bowl of salt, sugar, or whatever you're using to rim the glass. Let it dry for a moment, then shake any excess off over the sink. Fill your glass with mocktail, and you're good to go!

Cube it up.

Ice cubes aren't just practical—they can be pretty, too! Make your own colored cubes by adding food coloring. Display the colored cubes in a clear ice cooler at your party.

Make Your Own Sanding Sugar

For an extra twist, decorate your signature sip with custom-colored sanding sugar.

1 cup (240 mL) white or sanding sugar
food coloring
plastic bag with a seal

1. Place sugar and food coloring in bag. The amount of food coloring you use will depend on how dark you want the sugar to be.

2. Close the top of the bag. Knead until all the sugar is colored. Repeat if the sugar is not dark enough.

3. Spread colored sugar onto a plate or baking sheet until completely dry.

Optional: For an extra twist, choose one of the mix-ins on the right for your sanding sugar. Coordinate with your signature sip's flavor!

- cocoa or vanilla bean powder
- finely crushed hard candy
- sprinkles
- edible glitter
- light sprinkle of cayenne pepper, salt, or sour candy powder
- lemon, lime, or orange zest

27

Your Party Style

What's your party décor personality?
Take this quick quiz to find out:

You're at the party supply store. What catches your eye?

a) a brightly colored vase

b) a cool old chalkboard

c) a picnic basket with plaid trim

d) an oversized peacock feather centerpiece

Who's your style icon?

a) Taylor Swift

b) Zooey Deschanel

c) Rachel Bilson

d) Katy Perry

Your dream dinner party would be:

a) a modern around-the-world feast

b) a communal dinner in a cool barn

c) a lively backyard barbecue

d) an eight-course extravaganza

If you answered mostly A, you're **Bold and Bright**

If you answered mostly B, you're a **Classic Cutie**

If you answered mostly C, you're a **Down-Home Darling**

If you answered mostly D, you're a **Drama Queen** (in the best way, of course!)

Let The Games Begin!

If the fun starts to fizzle, pull out some popular party games. Have these time-tested faves standing by and ready to go.

Would You Rather?

With this game, you'll learn a lot about your friends in a little time! It's easy to play. All you have to do is ask gross, funny, or random questions. Everyone splits up into two sides depending on their answer to the question. For instance, ask, "Would you rather skip summer vacation or skip your birthday?" The vacation people would go to one side of the room and the b-day peeps to the other. It's fun to see what everyone says for each Q!

Handbag Hello

Split into teams. Ask everyone to take out her handbag—it plays a big part in this game! Once all the teams are ready, read out some items that might be found in a purse. List both common and unusual pocketbook treasures! Whichever team has the most total items between them gets the gold. If you've got boys and girls at your party, change the game to include backpacks or wallets.

The Fame Game

Tape an index card on each person's back with a famous person's name written on it. (Shh ... it's a secret!) All the players must then walk around asking yes-or-no questions to try to find out who they are. Great for getting people mingling and mixing!

Clean Sweep

Cleaning might not be your idea of fun, but it's a must before your party can take place. Stay organized with this thorough room-by-room checklist for gettin' it done!

(Helpful hint: space out the cleaning tasks the week before the party. Make it fun by rockin' out to some squeaky-clean tunes.)

All Rooms

- ☐ dust the windowsills and clean the windows
- ☐ vacuum carpets and rugs
- ☐ dust and clean surfaces

Kitchen

- ☐ wash the floor
- ☐ scrub the sink, stove, and fridge
- ☐ clean off cabinets
- ☐ do all dishes
- ☐ wipe down the tabletops/sinks

Bathroom(s)

- [ ] wash the floor
- [ ] scrub the sink, counter, and toilet
- [ ] clean the mirror
- [ ] wash shower curtain and rug (if necessary)

Bedroom(s)

- [ ] straighten up any clutter or clothes
- [ ] make the bed

Countdown to Fun

Just when you think you're done, something new almost always pops up! Find out how to handle last-minute tasks without getting frazzled.

- [ ] Pick out your serving pieces, dishes, and platters several days before the party. (Make sure to ask what's "off-limits" first.) Wash and set them aside for easy access. If you discover you don't have enough spoons or cups, now's the time to find or buy more.

- [ ] Label the bottom of any borrowed dishes or servingware with a piece of masking tape. The tape will remind you to return it.

- [ ] Make lists! It may seem tedious, but writing things down is the best way to keep a record. It's easier to see on paper how many dishes require forks or which can be prepared ahead of time.

- [ ] Do as much cooking as possible in the days leading up to the party. Make sure you label food so family members know that it's "hands off!"

- [ ] Keep track of what goes into each recipe. A guest with special dietary needs might need to know the ingredients. It might be helpful to label dishes in advance so your guests know what's safe.

☐ If a recipe doesn't turn out, keep cool. You can always buy a few pre-made items to have on hand.

☐ Follow the 80/20 rule if you start to get stressed. Focus on the most important 20 percent of a project, and the rest will take care of itself.

☐ Empty the dishwasher before the party starts. That way, you can load it as the party progresses. Nothing kills a party vibe like looking at dirty dishes!

☐ This is your party—don't let anyone pressure you into changing your plans. If someone asks if they can bring an uninvited guest, or if you can change your party time for them, it's OK to say no. You have enough to worry about without having to stress about your budget or party prep.

☐ Let the neighbors know you're expecting guests. It's only polite to let them know when and why your street will be busy! Ask them if there is anywhere they don't want your guests to walk or park.

Ready? 3...2...1...fun!

One-Stop Sweet Shoppe

Set your party apart with a decadent dessert table. A few simple recipes, crafts, and ideas can come together to create the ultimate tableful of sweets.

SIGNATURE STYLE:
CREATIVE CUPCAKE TOPPERS

DIVINE DECOR:
COORDINATING FABRIC TABLE RUNNER

OVER THE TOP:
PARTY POM-POMS

FAVORS (FOR NOW OR LATER):
CAKE POPS

Mash store-bought cupcakes (frosting and all) in a bowl until they form a dough. Roll into balls. Press a lollipop stick into each. Dip into melted candy melts. Decorate and let dry. Give each guest a small bouquet on their way out the door.

Party Pom-Poms

Draw your guests' eyes with these pretty-in-pink pom-poms. They'll add a colorful touch to unused space in your party room.

- one package (8 to 10 sheets) tissue paper
- fishing line
- scissors

1. Spread out tissue paper. Leave the paper in a stack.

2. Fold the tissue paper accordion-style. Fold the same direction as the original fold lines. Continue until the whole piece is folded into a strip.

3. Tie a loop of fishing line around the center of the tissue paper strip.

4. Cut the ends of the tissue paper in a curved shape. You can also cut them like an arrow.

5. Hold the tissue strip in the center. Fan one side of the tissue paper.

6. Gently pull the individual sheets of tissue paper apart, toward the middle of the paper. Alternate sides so your pom-pom is even.

7. Repeat on the other side. Fluff the pom-pom, as needed.

8. Tie a long piece of fishing line to the original loop. Use the long piece to hang your pom-pom.

Optional: Layer different shades of tissue paper to create an ombre effect. For example, for pink ombre you could use dark pink, light pink, and white.

Dip the tips of the tissue paper strip into colored water. Let them soak for a few minutes. Allow them to dry completely before fluffing.

Pretty Poms

There are many ways to display your pretty pom-poms.

- Hang pom-poms at varying heights over your tablescape. Use a single color for a subtle effect. Mix up shades and colors for a more dramatic look.

- For a prettier presentation, hang pom-poms with ribbon or thin strips of tulle.

- Pile pom-poms together for a large and fluffy centerpiece.

- Glue mini pom-poms to toothpicks for fun cupcake toppers.

- Bunch pom-poms together to create a chandelier. Add Chinese lanterns or balloons in contrasting colors for extra flair.

- Make pom-poms of various sizes. String them vertically, from largest to smallest.

The Big Idea

There's always a reason to celebrate! But sometimes the best parties are for no reason at all. Throwing a themed bash is a great way to show your creativity. It also gives you a reason to gather your BFFs just for the fun of it. Using a theme adds an extra layer of fun. It also gives your guests an idea of what to expect at the event.

Where can you find a killer theme idea? Let us count the ways! There are lots of resources to help spark a light bulb moment. Party-planning sites have whole sections devoted to different themes, color palettes, and designs. From darling décor to surprising sips, you'll find no shortage of inspiration!

 Find more downloadables and other party accessories at www.perfectpartiesguide.com

PARTY LIKE A ROCK STAR

Pump up the volume and take center stage with this rockin' party theme.

THE LOOK

To party like a star, you have to look the part. Ask your guests to dress like their favorite pop princess. Or challenge them to design their own diva look! Neon clip-on hair extensions, ripped jeans, and crazy prints are all fair game.

In-Style Invite

Who wouldn't love an all-access pass to your VIP bash? Spread the word with style. Hand out laminated backstage pass-style invites clipped on glittery lanyards.

Get Inked Here

Setting the Stage

Set up a mock tattoo parlor filled with bold body art stickers. Your friends will love comparing their temporary ink.

Paparazzi alert! Set up a table full of fun props such as boas, sunglasses, and inflatable guitars. Hang a sheet as a photo backdrop. Then ask a camera-savvy relative to take some shots of your friends posing. Or snap them with a cell phone to share them in an instant.

Eats and Treats

Live out loud with these killer microphone cupcakes!

- dark frosting
- colored cake cones
- baked cupcakes
- dark sugar sprinkles

Spread a thin layer of frosting inside the upper part of the cake cone. (This will help hold the cupcake in place.) Place the cupcake inside the cone, bottom-side-down. Frost the top of the cupcake. Roll the frosted cupcake in sprinkles.

*Tip: An ice cream cone cupcake baking rack will make frosting easier. If you can't find one, cut cone-sized holes in the bottom of a disposable roasting pan or cereal box. Then flip the pan upside down before setting a cupcake cone in each hole.

YOU'VE GOT GAME

Crank things up a notch by holding a battle of the air bands! Challenge your fellow rockers to show off their air guitar skills. You can even stage a tournament. Have your friends face off to see who's got star quality to spare. Try karaoke or band video games for another off-the-charts option.

Signature Sip: The Rock-Tail

This mocktail is destined to be a #1 hit!

- 4 tablespoons (60 milliliters) grenadine
- 16 ounces (.47 liters) ginger ale
- Pop Rocks
- lollipop

Mix grenadine with ginger ale. Serve in a martini glass rimmed with Pop Rocks. Garnish each glass with a lollipop.

Favors with Flair:

- neon plastic sunglasses
- custom playlist suggestions

 Look for more rockin' party downloads at www.perfectpartiesguide.com/themes/party-like-a-rock-star

TEA TIME

Why have tea for two when you can sip with a set of friends? Tip your pinky to this simply fabulous tea party!

THE LOOK

Pretty in pastel is the name of the game. Explore floral prints, elegant brooches, and strands of pearls. Ladylike looks are what tea party chic is all about. Give your guests white glove service with—what else?—white gloves!

In-Style Invite

Set the theme with teapot-shaped invitations. Choose classically girly patterns such as stripes, polka dots, flowers, and scallops.

Setting the Stage

Weather permitting, host your tea party outside in the backyard—ideally in the garden! Being outdoors will add an airy, festive feel.

Create a make-your-own-tea station where your besties can find their favorite flavor. Stock up on must-have tea blends such as jasmine, Earl Grey, herbal, and green.

Collect colorful teapots or dainty teacups to use as the table centerpieces. Set out place cards with your guests' names written in calligraphy.

Signature Sip: Honey Child

Not everyone loves hot tea, so why not offer something on the chill side too?

- ½ cup (120 mL) chilled green tea with honey and ginseng
- ¼ cup (60 mL) orange juice
- ¼ cup (60 mL) pineapple juice
- ½ cup (120 mL) ginger ale

Mix all the ingredients together. Serve over crushed ice for a refreshing beverage.

Favors with Flair:

- a variety of tea bags in a colorful sheer pouch
- lace frosted-glass tealight holders

YOU'VE GOT GAME

In Great Britain, high-styling Brits go out wearing funky hats called fascinators. Take a tip from the royals and have a fascinator-making contest! Set out elastic headbands, fabric glue, feathers, buttons, and other fun accessories. Whoever makes the most royally regal hat takes home a prize! Prize idea—the book *Tea with Jane Austen*.

Eats and Treats

Along with scones, pastries, and fresh fruit, finger sandwiches are absolutely a tea party must.

- cookie cutters
- white or wheat bread
- 1 pound (455 grams) of prepared chicken salad
- radish, thinly sliced
- cucumber, thinly sliced

Start by using cookie cutters to cut the bread into fun shapes, such as hearts, triangles, or stars. To make an open-face tea sandwich, spread chicken salad onto a piece of cut bread. Top with a thin slice of radish and cucumber. For extra decoration, use a small cookie cutter to decorate the sandwiches with tiny cucumber hearts and flowers.

Steep yourself in tea time tips at
www.perfectpartiesguide.com/themes/tea-time

PAMPER ME PRETTY

Why make a pricey trip to the spa? You can pamper with pals in the comfort of your own home!

THE LOOK

Comfort is the key! Tell your friends that the party is B.Y.O.B. (bring your own bathrobe.) Your friends will love lounging in their soft duds all day.

In-Style Invite

Hand out gift certificates for something great! Each certificate gives your guests entry to a super-exclusive spa—at your house! For an extra fun touch, do a creative spin on your last name and turn it into the "spa." Add a spa menu with all of the fun activities that your guests can look forward to taking part in.

Setting the Stage

Set the "me time" mood with scented candles, lots of floor pillows, and soothing music. Water pitchers and fresh fruit bowls will give your guests an extra-healthy punch.

Create various pampering stations. Each station should have different spa services your guests can indulge in. For the mani/pedi area, be sure to include nail art stickers, polishes, files, and buffers. A rose petal foot soak bowl is great for tired tootsies!

Eats and Treats

For food, focus on healthy bites such as cucumber finger sandwiches, fruit salad, and lettuce wraps. For dessert, go cutesy with these adorable and bite-sized "polish puffs!"

- pastel food coloring
- water or milk
- marshmallows
- chocolate frosting
- chocolate chews

Add food coloring to water or milk. Stir until food coloring is dissolved. Dip marshmallows into the colored liquid. Let dry. Dab some frosting onto one end of a chocolate chew. Press the frosting end into the center of each marshmallow so that it looks like a nail polish bottle. Arrange all of your puffs on a pretty platter and enjoy!

*Tip: For richer colors, dip the marshmallows into thinned frosting or candy melts.

Recipe: Foodie Facials

This makes a face mask good enough to eat!

- ⅓ cup (80 mL) cocoa powder
- ¼ cup (60 mL) raw honey
- 2 tablespoons (30 mL) mashed avocado

Combine all ingredients in a small bowl. Stir until creamy. Apply to the face for 15 minutes. Be sure to take pictures of everyone as masked mamas! Rinse with warm water. Make sure each guest has a towel for drying off.

Favors with Flair:

- handmade soaps
- flip-flops
- bottles of nail polish
- sleep masks

Signature Sip: All That Razz

Fruit-infused water is all the rage at fancy spas. One sip of this refreshing raspberry mocktail and you'll be saying, "Spaaahhh!"

Just the Essentials:
- sparkling water (plain or flavored)
- fresh raspberries
- sliced lemon

Pour water into a glass. Add up to six fresh raspberries and garnish with a slice of lemon. You can also buy a glass cooler and have your guests help themselves.

YOU'VE GOT GAME

Host a makeshift massage studio by having everyone stand in a circle. Each girl rubs the shoulders of the girl in front of her. Operation: relaxation in progress!

 Polish your party with favors, printables, and ideas from www.perfectpartiesguide.com/themes/pamper-me-pretty

A PIRATE P-ARRRRRTY

Shiver me timbers! This high sea shindig is sure to bring out the pirate in all of your best mates.

THE LOOK

Get pirate chic with bandannas, eye patches, vests, striped shirts, and tall boots. A parrot and a necklace of gold will only add to the outfit!

In-Style Invite

Set the tone for your buccaneer bash by writing the invite in pirate-speak! Get an instant cheat sheet by using an online pirate translator. You're sure to come up with something that even a landlubber will love. For a finishing touch, deliver your message in a bottle.

Setting the Stage

Make a mock treasure hunt by hiding gold coins, or pieces of eight, throughout the party area. Whoever collects the most loot wins the treasure to take home.

Every good party needs a dance break. Pump up your playlist with chart-topping tunes and let loose with a "pirates' booty" shake!

Hunt for more pirate party printables, recipes, and craft ideas at www.perfectpartiesguide.com/themes/a-pirate-p-arrrrrty

Eats and Treats

Use cocktail swords as mini skewers for fruits like pineapples, grapes, and blueberries. Plant a Jolly Roger in a bowl of crushed graham cracker sand. Serve round tortilla chips in a pirate's chest, and make them walk the plank into a bowl of salsa.

Favors with Flavor:

- chocolate gold coins
- a grab bag of "loot," such as bead necklaces and skull-and-crossbones jewelry
- eye patches

YOU'VE GOT GAME

Give an old game a new twist by starting a round of Capture the (Pirate) Flag. Head outside and split your group into two. Use a dividing line to clearly mark your territories. Each team gets a pirate flag to fiercely protect from pesky pillagers (aka the other team); both teams should also split into offense and defense.

Both sides have five minutes to hide their flag. After that, it's fair game for the other side to try to steal it. Anyone who gets tagged on enemy territory is out of the game – and off to walk the plank! But if someone can capture the flag and get it back to safe ground, the game is won and done.

Recipe: Treasure Island Cupcakes

- 1 box chocolate cake mix
- frosting
- graham crackers, crushed
- gold coins, rock candy, candy necklaces, and other small pieces of candy
- graham crackers, crushed

Follow directions on the box of cake mix for cupcakes. Let cool completely.

Frost cupcakes. Roll frosting in crushed graham crackers for a sandy look.

Decorate cupcakes with candy. Finish each one with a flag and a pirate-themed cupcake wrapper.

MOVIE UNDER THE STARS

Lights, camera, action! A backyard movie night is the perfect excuse to lay out under the stars. Grab a blanket, and watch a classic in the company of your real-life co-stars.

THE SET-UP

Bringing the big screen to your backyard isn't as hard as you might think. Don't spend money on an outdoor movie screen. Instead, use a wall or tie a large white sheet to two trees or poles. You'll also need a portable DVD projector to show the flick on your screen of choice. For seating, set up a bunch of comfy blankets, beanbags, or lawn chairs. Finally, light some citronella candles to keep the bugs at bay!

Setting the Stage

With this party, timing is everything! You'll want to start the movie as soon as it gets dark, so invite everyone to arrive just before dusk. That will provide plenty of time for chatting, noshing, and getting cozy before the big flick.

Make your party pop-ular! Set up a popcorn bar with tons of trimmings and toppings. Offer staples like kettle corn, white cheddar popcorn, and classic butter. For those with truly daring taste buds, set out plain popcorn and an array of toppings. Test out dry ranch powder, caramel syrup, or spicy sriracha sauce.

Go the extra mile with props like movie reels, a production slate, and striped popcorn boxes. Create a "Walk of Fame" down your driveway using large stars with your friends' names on them.

In-Style Invite

That's the ticket! Pass out an adorable invite in the style of an "Admit One" movie stub! Make your own or browse the many styles available online.

50

Eats and Treats

Along with the popcorn bar, consider setting up a concession stand for traditional faves like licorice, candy bars, and nuts. Choose soft pretzels and hot dogs for more filling treats.

Now Showing—The Classics

If you've seen all the latest flicks and are looking for something classic, stop here! Some can't-miss girlfriend picks include:

- *Breakfast at Tiffany's* (1961)
- *Casablanca* (1942)
- *National Velvet* (1944)
- *Clueless* (1995)
- *Grease* (1978)
- *Singin' in the Rain* (1952)
- *Gone With The Wind* (1939)
- *Some Like It Hot* (1959)
- *West Side Story* (1961)
- *Say Anything …* (1989)
- *A League Of Their Own* (1992)
- *10 Things I Hate About You* (1999)
- *Pitch Perfect* (2012)

Favors with Flair:

- popcorn balls
- big sunglasses and feather boas
- mini trophies that look like Oscars

Signature Sip: Cola Queen

Go classic Hollywood with a Roy Rogers or a Shirley Temple—but add a limey twist! These soda-based sips put a fun spin on this classic movie beverage.

- 1 tablespoon (15 mL) grenadine
- 1 tablespoon (15 mL) lime juice
- 1 can of soda (cola for a Roy Rogers, lemon-lime for a Shirley Temple)

Combine all ingredients in a tall glass and enjoy! For extra flair, add star-shaped straw toppers or crushed ice.

YOU'VE GOT GAME

Movie trivia time–test your besties on just how well they know their fave flicks. Whoever gets the most correct answers snags a pair of movie tickets or a DVD!

 Watch for more movie night munchies, downloads, and party ideas at www.pcrfectpartiesguide.com/themes/movie-under-the-stars

YOU'VE GOT GAME

Here's a real winner—a mystery box game night. No need to roll the dice on whether your guests will have fun. This party is a sure bet!

In-Style Invite

Forget the Queen of Hearts. You'll be the queen of invites with this deck of cards. Print out the party info onto brightly colored cardstock. Then glue the info onto the back of a giant playing card.

Setting the Stage

Since you'll be sitting around a table why not use a nifty nameplate? Mark each person's spot with a personalized nametag. Stick to the theme and use Scrabble tiles to spell out each name. You can also use this trick for labeling eats and treats at the food table. •••••••••••••••••

Deck the walls with lots of game boards! From Monopoly to Life, board games make awesome wall hangings. And the creativity doesn't stop there—what about using a Twister mat as a tablecloth? For a dessert table centerpiece, pay tribute to Go Fish with a festive fishbowl. •••••••••••

Would your friends do anything for money? There's only one way to find out! As they arrive, hand each person $200 in Monopoly money. During the party, people can bribe each other to do silly things in exchange for dough. Whoever has the most moolah at the end gets a prize! •••••••••••

Eats and Treats

Set up a "Candy Crush Corner." Fill mason jars with treats such as hard candies, gumdrops, and swirly lollipops. Let your friends "combine" candies by bagging their favorites for later.

Signature Sip: Apples to Apples

Be the apple of everyone's eye with this sparkling signature sip!

- 1 bottle sparkling apple cider
- 1 cup (240 mL) cranberry juice
- ½ cup (120 mL) orange juice

Stir all ingredients together, and serve. Use red and green cups topped with brown straws to really pull the theme together.

YOU'VE GOT GAME

Popular Indoor Games:

SCENE IT!
MONOPOLY
CLUE
CATCHPHRASE
TABOO
SCATTERGORIES

Awesome Outdoor Games:

BEANBAG TOSS
LADDER GOLF
BOCCE
THREE-LEGGED RACE
WATER BALLOON PIÑATA
FRISBEE GOLF
LAWN TWISTER

Take indoor games outside! Make life-sized versions of these classic games. Use balls, balloons, boxes, Frisbees, and large pieces of cardboard to recreate game pieces.

DON'T BREAK THE ICE   HI HO CHERRY-O
PING-PONG   CONNECT FOUR
JENGA   BANANAGRAMS
PICTIONARY

Favors with Flavor:

- Mad Libs books
- fuzzy dice
- deck of cards

 Roll for more game night ideas, printables, and party tips at www.perfectpartiesguide.com/themes/you-ve-got-game

'STACHE BASH

It's true—mustaches are the new trendy accessories. Tip your hat to these funky face decorations with a mustache bash!

THE LOOK

Clearly, the most important accessory is the mustache. Your choice: You can buy stick-on mustaches or make mustaches-on-a-stick for those who prefer a more temporary transformation! Bow ties and berets can help complete the look.

Setting the Stage

Have family photos around the house? Give everyone a mini-makeover by using a black dry-erase marker to put 'staches on each pic. Test that the marker is removable first!

Taking picture proof of the mustache makeover is half the fun! Set up a simple photo booth for your guests to use. Grab a large, colorful photo frame and a camera. Your friends will go to town showing off their fabulous facial hair.

 'Stache some party ideas for later by visiting www.perfectpartiesguide.com/themes/stache-bash

Eats and Treats

Printables are the secret to turning your treats table into mustache madness. Add mustache toppers to striped straws with a nearby sign reading "Wet Your Whiskers." Stick mustaches on items like candles, cups, or bottles. Make mustache-shaped sandwiches or cookies. Watch out—things might start to get hairy!

Signature Sip: Peach Fuzz

You don't need a stiff upper lip to drink this smooth concoction! This recipe will make enough for 12 guests.

- 9 cups (2 liters) soda water
- 3 cups (.7 L) peach juice
- 3 cups (.7 L) sparkling white grape juice
- peach or mango sorbet
- striped paper straws

Combine all ingredients in a pitcher, then pour into glasses. Garnish each glass with a scoop of sorbet and a straw to keep your 'stache clean.

Favors with Flavor:

- party "stash" of 'stache-shaped treats
- scented shaving cream
- mustache-shaped temporary tattoos
- mustache-shaped chocolates

YOU'VE GOT GAME

Pin the Tail on the Donkey is a classic kid game. Add mustaches for a modern twist. Grab a poster of your favorite actor or pop star. Each person gets a chance to pin the 'stache on the star. Add a blindfold and a few spins to make the game even harder.

Mustache Cookies

1 roll refrigerated
   sugar cookie
   dough
1/3 cup (80 mL)
   cocoa powder
baking sheet

parchment paper
cookie sticks
1 can frosting
milk
sugar sprinkles

Combine dough and cocoa powder until thoroughly mixed. Roll out dough to about .25 inches (.6 cm) thick.

Use mustache cookie cutters to cut out the dough. Set cookies onto a baking sheet lined with parchment paper.

Gently insert a stick into each cookie. (Place each stick slightly off-center for the most stability.) Patch any cracks with extra dough. Pinch the dough around the stick to make sure it's secure.

Bake cookies according to directions on the package. Let cool completely.

Thin frosting with milk until frosting is easily spreadable. Cover cookies with frosting. Press cookies frosting-side-down into a plate of sprinkles to coat thoroughly.

*Tip: For extra salty 'staches, chop up two pieces of cooked bacon. Add your bacon bits to the dough before baking.

PARTY GRAS

Why travel to New Orleans for Mardi Gras? Bring a slice of the South to your own cool Carnival.

THE LOOK

Purple, gold, and green are the traditional Mardi Gras colors. Encourage your guests to sport those shades. Go big with a jester hat. Rock wild beads to truly look like you fit in at the French Quarter.

Setting the Stage

It's not really a Mardi Gras masquerade until everyone has a mask. Set up a make-your-own-mask station where guests can accessorize and get artsy. Have eye masks, 10-inch (25-centimeter) wooden sticks, sequins, feathers, and glue. You can also purchase mask-making kits online.

Lively jazz fills the streets at Mardi Gras, so be sure to reflect that with your playlist! Check out classics like Fats Domino or Louis Armstrong. Brass bands, Cajun, and zydeco music are always good choices. (Don't leave "When The Saints Go Marching In" off your list!) If you're still stumped, you can type "Mardi Gras" into any music app, and it will do the work for you.

 Parade to the web to find more Party Gras ideas at www.perfectpartiesguide.com/themes/party-gras

Recipe: Muffuletta Kabobs

The muffuletta is a staple in New Orleans kitchens. Give your guests a bite-sized taste of this monster-sized sandwich.

- wooden skewers
- loaf of Italian bread, cut into cubes
- salami, cut into cubes
- whole green olives (reserve 2 tablespoons (30 mL) olive juice)
- ham, cut into cubes
- provolone cheese, cut into cubes
- 3 tablespoons (45 mL) olive oil
- 2 tablespoons (30 mL) red wine vinegar
- dried oregano

Thread pieces of bread, salami, olives, ham, and cheese onto a skewer. Repeat until all ingredients are used.

In a small bowl, combine olive juice, olive oil, and red wine vinegar. Brush lightly over all the skewers. Refrigerate up to a day in advance. Sprinkle with oregano before serving.

Signature Sip: Big Easy Slush

This sensational sip is a New Orleans favorite! It looks good and it tastes good. Celebrate by pouring yourself a glass.

- purple sports drink
- green sports drink
- yellow sports drink

Freeze each color drink in its own ice cube tray. Once the cubes are frozen, use a blender to crush each color cubes into slushes. Layer the slushes into clear glasses.

Favors with Flavor:

The party may be over, but you can send your guests home with some classy coasters to continue the fun.

- a coaster
- pencil
- felt
- scissors
- Mardi Gras bead necklaces
- fabric glue

Use a coaster to trace a circle onto felt. Cut the circle out.

Take a necklace and cut it so it's no longer a circle. Add a drop of glue to the center of the felt circle. Press one end of the necklace into the glue. Spiral the beads around the center, adding more glue as you go. Let dry completely.

SHine on

Turn off the lights and turn on the fun with this glowing gathering!

THE LOOK

Four letters say it all – n-e-o-n! Glow-in-the-dark gear or white colors will stand out against the darkness of your evening event. Decorate with neon acrylic paint and glow sticks. Give your guests neon body paint for extra oomph.

In-Style Invite

Make an oh-so-bright invite with glow sheets and glow-in-the-dark markers.

*Tip: Make these invites outside. The glow sheets smell!

Setting the Stage

Décor plays a big part in making this party light up. Put glow sticks inside balloons and beach balls and place them around the party. Stick glow-in-the-dark stars to the ceiling and walls, and hang a crepe paper chandelier. If budget permits, buy or rent a few blacklights for a look your guests will surely "rave" about!

Got a digital camera? Get ready to be a shiny shutterbug! Turn your camera to the lowest shutter speed. Set the camera on a tripod and click. Use glow sticks to wave shapes or write words in the air. The pattern you draw will show up in the final photo.

Light up your party with extra projects, recipes, and downloads at www.perfectpartiesguide.com/themes/shine-on

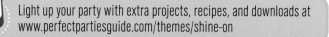

Favors with Flair:

- glow jewelry
- LED sunglasses
- glow in the dark nail polish
- neon plastic sunglasses in cool shapes

Signature Sip: Lite Brite

Make your hair stand on-end with this radioactive refresher!

- glow stick
- tall plastic cup
- shorter clear plastic cup
- clear soda

Turn on your glow stick and bend it so that it fits in the bottom of the tall cup. Place the shorter cup inside the tall cup so that it rests on the glow stick. Fill the shorter cup with soda and light up your world!

Eats and Treats

Create some contrast at your treats table by using neon cups and plates against a black tablecloth. (Add a few blacklight candles for effect!) Let glowing gelatin do double duty as both a decoration and a delicious treat.

- green gelatin
- 1 cup (240 mL) boiling water
- wire whisk
- 1 cup (240 mL) tonic water
- jars

Pour the gelatin packet into a large bowl, and add boiling water. Stir for two minutes using a wire whisk, then pour tonic water into the mixture. Continue to stir. After it cools, pour into the jars. Place your gelatin jars in the refrigerator for three hours or until set. Place the jars on the table under a blacklight and let them glow!

YOU'VE GOT GAME

Get your glow on with a game of glow tag. In this game, everyone loosely ties a glow stick around his or her belt loop (or wrist). Whoever is "it" must capture each glow stick. The people who lose their glow sticks must go over to the "other" side and help get the remaining players. Last glow stick standing wins!

59

CRAZY CARNIVAL

Step right up! This party is full of Ferris wheel-sized fun! It may not be the big top, but it's sure to be a big success.

THE LOOK

Go traditional with red and white stripes to represent the Big Top. Circus music, popcorn and sugary snacks, and carnival games will ensure your party is the biggest amusement around.

Setting the Stage

Set up a guessing games area where your guests can put their skills to the test! A tried-and-true fave is a "Count the Jelly Beans" jar. For something different, use pennies or popcorn. For more fun, make a "Guess That Grin" board. Fill it with closely-cropped pictures of celeb smiles. Then have your guests try to figure out who's who.

Recreate carnival faves with fun themed food containers around the party. A container of chocolate kisses can be the "Kissing Booth." Place it next to a bowl of colorful lip glosses for your guests.

Buy cheap vases at the dollar store and wrap them in red carnival tickets. Fill the vases with bright flowers and pinwheels. Don't forget to get helium balloons! A container of homemade fortune cookies can serve as the "Fortune Teller."

Signature Sip: Cotton Club

Newsflash! Cotton candy can easily become a super-sweet drink. Set pink cotton candy in a glass and pour lime sparkling water over the top. It's candy for the eyes and the tastebuds!

Favors with Flair:

For a fun favor idea, buy white and pink tea lights for each guest. With an adult's help, carefully melt just the tops of the tea lights. Sprinkle small, round rainbow sprinkles over the wax before it hardens. Hand the candles out with small bags of frosted animal crackers.

YOU'VE GOT GAME

This game is sure to lift your guests' spirits up, up, and away! Have a balloon twisting contest to see who can come up with the craziest creations. Afterward, display them all or wear them as goofy hats. Other game ideas include hula-hoop contests and a pie-eating challenge.

Eats and Treats

Fun presentation is the secret to carnival cuteness. Try putting caramel corn in polka-dotted paper cones, or use pinwheels as cupcake toppers. Keep colors bright and cheerful!

Create a hot dog station where guests can dress up their dogs with all the trimmings. Use gingham placemats or napkins to add an extra down-home touch to the table.

 Hit the big top with bonus crafts, recipes, and downloads at www.perfectpartiesguide.com/themes/crazy-carnival

THEME-O-RAMA

Haven't gotten your fill of fun party themes yet? Here's a list of more ideas to get your hostess wheels turning.

Murder Mystery

Whodunnit? Put on your sassiest detective hat and invite friends over for a night of intrigue. As far as party prep, buying a themed murder mystery kit is your best bet. Most kits include everything from the storyline to character descriptions to props.

Medal Madness

The Olympics may only happen every few years, but you can go for the gold with an Olympic-themed party any time! Assign each guest a country, and encourage everyone to dress the part. "Events" can include a flag decorating contest and games like water balloon toss and Twister. Don't forget to award medals!

Snowflake Dazzle

Cozy up with a winter party. Decorate with lots of silver, white, and strings of holiday light. Keep everyone warm with a cider or hot cocoa bar. Once everyone is nice and toasty, get together to make homemade snow globes with mason jars. Send each guest home with supplies and instructions on how to finger knit their own scarf.

To get more ideas for Theme-o-Rama parties, visit www.perfectpartiesguide.com/party-of-the-month

Bookworm Bash

Choose your favorite popular series to celebrate. Have everyone bring a copy of their favorite book to compare, or host a trivia contest. Ask guests to dress as their favorite character. Serve food mentioned in the book. Make rolls or mockingjay cookies for a Hunger Games party. Find pumpkin juice, onion soup, or treacle tart recipes to celebrate Harry Potter. Hand out book covers or bookmarks for favors. Then ask your friends for suggestions for your next bookworm bash!

Otaku Party

Turn up the J-pop and greet your guests with "kon'nichiwa!" Send out origami or mini manga invites. Challenge attendees to dress in Harajuku style, or dare them to show up in their cutest kigurumi. Serve bento boxes while watching everyone's favorite anime flicks. Decorate cupcakes with frosted cherry blossoms, or top them with a round, red sprinkle to represent the Japanese flag. Send guests home with a pair of their own chopsticks.

Color Coded

What's your favorite color? Why not celebrate it? Coordinate your party accessories to find the perfect hues. Play with food coloring to create an unforgettable ombre cake. Hit the paper product aisle to make table runners, banners, and party pom-poms to hang from the ceiling. For extra fun, mash up your color theme with another party idea. Decorate in blue and play blues music. Choose orange for a fall theme. Or reduce, reuse, and recycle at a green party!

Beat the Heat

Invite your friends to bring their suits and towels to your wet and wild party. Serve ice-cold juice boxes, frozen treats, and jugs of flavored water to stay hydrated. Have buckets full of water balloons ready to throw. (Add food coloring or glitter for extra flair!) Send each guest home with squirt guns or beach balls for lots of future fun.

Rag Swap

Imagine going shopping without spending a dime. If that sounds too good to be true, think again. A rag swap allows everyone to bring gently used clothing items and shoes for fresh and fun exchange. How does it work? For each item you bring, you get to pick one from the pile. Whatever doesn't get picked gets donated to charity. Everybody wins! For food, keep the theme going by swapping cookie recipes.

Happy Bark-day!

Come. Sit. Stay! Celebrate everyone's best friend with a puppypalooza! Set up a treat bar and let pooches take their favorites home in a doggy bag. Play bobbing for hot dogs or Simon Says. Serve snacks in dog bowls (puppy chow, anyone?) Give your guests stuffed dogs with adoption certificates for favors they'll remember forever.

To get more ideas for Theme-o-Rama parties, visit
www.perfectpartiesguide.com/party-of-the-month

Morning Mania

Don't want to wait for the party to start? Get everyone moving by hosting a morning party! Chow down on pancake pops and freshly squeezed orange juice, or set up a donut decorating bar. Have guests show up in their jammies. (Tell them to bring sleeping bags for breakfast "in bed!")

Gardening Guests

Savor the springtime with an outdoor gardening party. Choose floral patterns or gingham and denim to set the scene. Let guests decorate terra-cotta pots and then plant their favorite flowers inside. Add fairy garden accessories for an extra-special touch. Nibble on carrot cake cupcakes baked in tiny pots and vegetables in every color of the rainbow.

Art with Heart

Not your everyday crafting get-together! Bring out the inner artist by hosting a painting party. You provide the supplies, canvas or paper, and the space. All your guests need to bring is their creativity! Hand out cupcakes in paint plates with different sprinkles in each mixing well. Assign each person a famous painting to recreate. Donate your finished masterpieces to a local children's hospital.

Make and Take

Putting your special stamp on your shindig is as easy as three little letters: C-I-Y! (Craft It Yourself!)

Sure, making your own stuff can be time-consuming and stressful. But in the end, your party's one-of-a-kind flair will make it all worth it. Your guests will know how much work you put into throwing the most perfect party ever.

Get the skinny on perfecting projects such as crepe paper chandeliers, dipped pretzel rods, origami lanterns, and oh-so-sassy soaps. By mastering these favors, you'll take the party to the next level of fun!

 Find more decorations, favors, and other craft projects at www.perfectpartiesguide.com

Hitting the Right Note

Hey, Miss DJ! Making custom playlists for the party can be half the fun. Find out how to get in tune with your guests:

- Try to pick tunes that suit your theme. Big band swing tunes or funky reggae are great examples of ways to liven up the party vibe. Throw in some classics that everyone will know for good measure.

- Make sure your playlist will last the whole party. Having hours of preselected music means one less thing to think about.

- If you have friends coming over to help set up, time their arrival with their favorite tunes. Sara's coming an hour early? Move her jam to the front of the line.

- Don't have time to load up your MP3 player? Consider using a free music service. All you have to do is type in a keyword (such as "Taylor Swift" or "jazz"), and the playback will be a custom collection of music to your liking! Now that's music to our ears.

Keep it familiar. Don't try to impress guests with an obscure playlist. Stick with what people know. If you need to throw in something unusual, sandwich it between well-known favorites.

KEEP THE VOLUME IN CONTROL! MAKE SURE IT'S LOUD ENOUGH FOR PEOPLE TO HEAR, BUT SOFT ENOUGH TO CARRY ON CONVERSATIONS.

Insta-Atmosphere: Quick Tricks

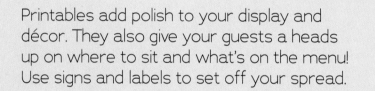

Create a DIY table runner using pretty wrapping paper. Layer two or more colors or patterns for more depth. Scatter vase gems or flat glass marbles over the top for some glittery color.

Printables add polish to your display and décor. They also give your guests a heads up on where to sit and what's on the menu! Use signs and labels to set off your spread.

Play with lighting to provide an instant room makeover. Switch out regular lightbulbs for ones with color, or simply dim the lights to add a bit of mood lighting. String lights are also a quick fix for soft lighting.

Scented candles and tealights create extra ambiance around the party. For a safer choice, use battery-powered LED tea lights or candles.

A balloon wall will make your party pop! Tape balloons of all different colors and designs on a big wall. String balloons onto a banner and write giant letters on them to spell out your theme. Fill white balloons with colored confetti or bits of tissue paper before blowing them up. Or go extra-large with huge round balloons!

 For more tips on shaping your party's atmosphere, visit www.perfectpartiesguide.com/tips

Tiny Treats: Favors That Rock

Favors are a way to send your guests home with a small memento of your party. They can be simple things that can be eaten or used right away. Or they can be objects guests will treasure for years to come.

Wrap candy or small trinkets, such as jewelry or toys, in tulle. Tie with colorful ribbons and decorate with a special charm.

Personalize mini jars of jam with fabric and string. Choosing fun fabrics and colors will make your favor that much sweeter!

 For more favor ideas, visit www.perfectpartiesguide.com

Make whimsical bubble wands by mixing ½ cup (120 mL) dishwashing liquid, 2 cups (480 mL) water, 2 teaspoons (10 mL) sugar, glitter, and food coloring. Divide bubble mix into small containers with bubble wands.

Give "green" a new meaning with tiny trees. Send each guest home with a seedling to plant in their own yard. They'll remember your party for years to come.

Give each guest a bundle of glow sticks tied together with glow-in-the-dark tape.

Find origami patterns that match your party theme. Give your guests their own origami figure. Or, better yet, send them home with origami paper and instructions on how to fold their own!

Nifty Nails

Leave a lasting impression with pretty polish! Let your guests go wild creating their own custom polishes.

- powdered eye shadows
- toothpick
- 3-inch (7.6-centimeter) square pieces of parchment paper
- clear nail polish
- glitter (optional)
- 4.5-millimeter ball bearings

1. Select your desired shade(s) of eye shadow. Use the toothpick to scrape eye shadow onto a piece of parchment paper.

2. Press the eye shadow between two pieces of parchment paper to grind into a fine powder.

3. Roll the parchment paper into a tight funnel. Use it to pour the eye shadow powder into the polish bottle.

4. Use a toothpick to stir the eye shadow into the polish.

5. Add glitter, if desired.

6. Add two or three ball bearings to the bottle. The ball bearings will help the polish mix evenly before each use.

FOR MORE CUSTOMIZATION, TRY:

- adding a drop or two of essential oil, fragrance oil, or food flavorings, such as vanilla or orange. Your nails will look and smell great!

- using shaped glitter that matches your party theme.

- using a label-making program to design custom labels for your polish bottles.

- using food coloring instead of eye shadow for a neon effect. (Use a clear base coat before applying, to avoid staining your fingers.)

Lovely Lace

Use your new polish to give your nails a lacy look.

1. Paint the bottom half of each finger at an angle.

2. Use a toothpick to create scalloped patterns along the top edge of the polish.

3. Accent the tip of your nail with silver polish.

4. Finish with clear nail polish.

Hot Rods

A good hostess never gets salty-unless she's prepping pretzels! Dipped pretzel rods are an easy and fun way to impress your guests. From chocolate to caramel, there are plenty of sugary coatings to pair with pretzels.

Chocolate Dippers

1 cup (240 mL) chocolate chips
1 tablespoon (15 mL) vegetable oil

Caramel Coated

½ pound (255 grams) soft caramels
2 tablespoons (30 mL) cream

Instructions for both:

1. Place ingredients in a microwave-safe bowl and heat for 30 seconds. Remove bowl and stir. Repeat until coating is completely melted and smooth.

2. Dip a pretzel rod into the coating, leaving the last third of the pretzel uncovered.

3. While the coating is still wet, roll pretzel in topping of your choice. For extra flair, drizzle colored candy melts over topped pretzel rods.

GO BEYOND NUTS AND SPRINKLES! FOR GOURMET COMBOS, TRY:

- white chocolate chips and chopped dried cranberries

- peanuts, mini marshmallows, and mini chocolate chips

- shredded coconut, crushed banana chips, and almonds

- a layer of caramel, a layer of chocolate, and chopped pecans

Get Crafty

Make your pretzels part of your party theme! Re-dip the very tips in colored candy melts to turn them into paintbrushes for arts and crafts.

Coat them with silver sugar for wands for wizard bashes. Decorate with star-shaped sprinkles to make scepters for princess parties.

Crepe Expectations

Add a touch of insta-glam with a shower of streamers. This colorful crepe paper chandelier is a simple yet stylish project. It's sure to make your party décor pop.

All the Essentials:

- measuring tape
- crepe paper in different colors
- hole punch

- double-sided tape
- 1 12-inch (30.5 cm) embroidery hoop
- ribbon or twine

1. Decide where to hang your chandelier. Use a measuring tape to decide how long the streamers should be. Once you have settled on a length, cut a streamer twice your measurement.

2. Measure and cut enough streamers to cover half the hoop.

3. Punch a line of circles along the edges of the crepe paper. The holes should be about 1 inch (2.5 cm) apart.

4. Stick a piece of double-sided tape around the inside of the embroidery hoop. Wrap the top part of a streamer around it so that it sticks to the tape.

5. Tape the end of the streamer to the opposite side of the embroidery hoop.

6. Repeat steps 4 and 5 until you've worked your way around the hoop. Use as many streamers as you like until you have the look you want.

7. Cut three pieces of ribbon or twine to 18-inch (46 cm) lengths. Evenly space each ribbon around the hoop. Tie the ribbon to the hoop, in between the streamers.

8. Knot the three ribbons together in the center of the hoop. Use them to hang the chandelier.

Adding Drama

Why stop at one? Use 8-inch (20 cm) embroidery hoops to make two smaller chandeliers. Hang one on either side of the larger chandelier.

Use self-adhesive gemstones to give the chandelier some extra glitz.

Karaoke Queens

Setting up a karaoke station will get all of your guests in (lip) sync. Let everyone release their rock star side with these ideas for simple karaoke setup.

- Download a karaoke app for instant access to tunes. All you have to do is plug your phone into the TV and start singing.

- If you want to really rock the mic, buy a microphone! Some microphones plug right into your music player. You can sing songs from your own music library or the mic's collection. Others let you record performances so that your party guests can remember their rock star moment after the party ends.

- Don't forget to make your karaoke "club" feel funky! Add a zebra-striped rug or lay a piano keyboard-style runner under the TV. Hang zig-zag accordion streamers from the ceiling as a backdrop. Disco or strobe lights will also help set the stage for your friends to take the spotlight.

 Download song request slips at www.perfectpartiesguide.com/downloads/karaoke-queens

Song Selection

Be prepared for guests to call dibs on "their" song. If two of your guests pick the same solo, suggest they sing it together.

For maximum crowd participation, pick songs that everyone can sing along to!

Keep the songs on the shorter side. Songs with long openings or instrumental breaks (such as "American Pie," "Thriller," or "Bohemian Rhapsody") can bring the room's energy down. Four minutes or less is a good starting point.

Unless you're a karaoke pro, avoid rap or songs that use Autotune.

Take a number! Have karaoke request slips available so your friends can get their faves on the list.

SONG SLIP

NAME:

SONG:

Share and Share Alike

Rule number one: Don't hog the mic! Make sure everyone who wants to sing takes a turn. An easy way to avoid a stage hog is to set rules before the party starts. For example, everyone has to sing at least once before someone gets to go again. Or have guests draw numbers so everyone has to wait their turn.

Extra Applause!

Karaoke is about having fun! Self-conscious guests may feel nervous about singing in front of a crowd. Help them feel at ease by having familiar tunes available, or offering to be their backup. Get your audience on board, too! A pumped-up crowd will help even the shyest singer open up.

On that note, don't force a timid singer to take a turn. If they want to sing, they'll put in their own song request.

T.G.G. TOTALLY GORGEOUS GUESTBOOK

Scrapbooks can capture moments in time, but a guestbook can provide a totally different type of memory. While pictures are worth a thousand words, a guest's heartfelt note is worth a mint to a hard-working hostess!

Props That Pop

Actual books are so yesterday. Why not have your guests sign a fun prop that matches your theme? Hit the right note for a music-themed shindig with a fake guitar or other instrument, or use a globe for an around-the-world party. Use a metallic marker for an extra dash of flair!

Totally Puzzled

Not sure what to do for a guestbook? Problem solved: puzzle it up! Blank puzzles are affordable to buy and make one-of-a-kind mementos. Before the shindig, put all of the puzzle pieces in a cute bowl or jar on the welcome table. As guests arrive, ask them to choose a piece, sign a message and place it where it belongs in the puzzle. (Give a prize to the guest who places the final piece!)

Chalk It Up

Photos are a quiet moment in time. What if they could actually talk? A camera, printer, and chalkboard can truly get their message across! Have your guests write messages on the chalkboard and take goofy photos of themselves holding it. After they're done, they can tack the photos onto a corkboard or tape them into your guestbook.

Smart Cookie

Calling all cookies-and-cream cuties! Chocolate cookie lovers will flip over this trendy way to celebrate their fave treat. Forget dunking these babies in milk—after all, dressing them up is much more fun.

- lollipop sticks
- chocolate sandwich cookies
- wax paper
- baking sheet
- 6 1-ounce (30-gram) white chocolate baking squares
- 1 teaspoon (5 mL) canola oil
- sprinkles

Tip: Use a chunk of craft foam to display the cookie pops. Place in a fancy container or wrap the outside with washi tape, tulle, or ribbon to dress it up.

1. Insert a lollipop stick into the center filling of a cookie. Place the cookie on a baking sheet lined with wax paper. Repeat until all cookies have a stick. Freeze the cookie pops for 10 minutes.

2. Melt the white chocolate in the microwave. Stir in the canola oil once chocolate is fully melted.

3. Remove the cookie pops from the freezer. Dip them one at a time in the melted chocolate. Make sure the cookie is evenly coated on both sides.

4. Top each cookie with sprinkles. Return to baking sheet and let dry completely.

Mix It Up

The simple dip is just the tip of the creative iceberg. Use different types of cookies, coatings, and toppings to suit your party!

- For game night, use food coloring to dye cookies to match a Twister mat or checkers board.

- Coat mini cookies with gold sprinkles or edible glitter to make pirate coins.

- Top each pop with sugar or fondant flowers for a spa treat.

- Dip only half the cookie to make fancy finger food for a tea party.

- Animal crackers are perfect for a circus theme. Press a whole cracker into the melted chocolate. Then decorate the cookie with rainbow sprinkles.

- Use glow sticks instead of lollipop sticks for a glow-in-the-dark event.

- Chocolate transfer sheets with a mustache design are the perfect addition for a 'stache bash.

Good Clean Fun

Who doesn't love suds? Your spa party will never fizzle with these surprising handmade soaps.

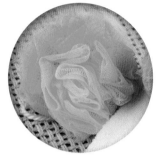

- 6 glycerin soap base cubes, about 1.5 to 2 ounces (43 to 57 grams) each
- 3 microwave-safe bowls
- fragrance oil

- soap dye in three colors
- soap mold
- spray bottle
- rubbing alcohol
- plastic wrap

1. Place two cubes of soap in a microwave-safe container. Microwave for 30 seconds. Stir, and then heat for another 30 seconds. Continue until completely melted. Watch container carefully to make sure that the base does not boil over.

2. Add fragrance oil and one color of dye. Stir until fully combined.

3. Pour mixture into soap mold. Spray with rubbing alcohol. The alcohol will remove any bubbles that rise to the surface. Let sit 10 minutes, or until a skin forms.

4. Repeat steps 1–2 with a second container of soap and a second color dye. Pour over the first layer of soap. Spray with rubbing alcohol.

5. Repeat steps 1–2 with a third container of soap and a third color dye. Pour over the second layer of soap. Spray with rubbing alcohol.

6. Let soap harden at least three hours. Remove from the molds, and cover with plastic wrap.

Dress It Up

Plastic wrap will protect your soap from drying out, but it's not the prettiest packaging. Dress up your soaps to complete your pampering party.

- Use a tulle favor bag. Thread a bead or small charm onto the ribbon that ties the bag shut.

- Cover each bar in wrapping paper. Then decorate the bar with ribbon or raffia.

- Nestle soap in Chinese take-out boxes packed with tissue paper or colored shredded paper.

Lay It On

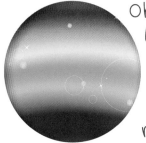

Oh, sugar, are you in for a treat! Layered drinks look and taste magical. Want your bevvies to rock the rainbow look? Here's the trick—the amount of sugar in each drink is what keeps it separate in the glass. Successful drink layering means working your way up the sugary ladder.

Top – beverage that is sugar-free or has the least sugar
Middle – beverage with less sugar than the bottom beverage
Bottom – beverage with the highest sugar content

Directions:

1. Fill a glass with ice cubes.

2. Pour the bottom layer into the glass. Fill the glass about one-third of the way full.

3. Pour the second layer in very slowly. If the beverage comes out too fast, use the back of a spoon to slow the pour.

4. Pour the top layer of liquid to the top of the glass. Garnish, if desired.

Super Sips

Try layering these combinations:

- cranberry juice, lemon-lime soda, blue sports drink
- berry-blend juice, lemonade, berry-flavored iced tea
- cherry juice, pineapple juice, orange juice
- kiwi syrup, lemonade, watermelon juice
- grenadine, passion fruit juice, club soda

Light-Up Lantern

Light up your world with a string of origami lights. Find out how to fold your way to funky handmade décor.

- 6-inch (15-cm) square origami paper
- string of Christmas lights

1. Begin with the paper colored side up. Fold the paper in half in both directions, then unfold. Turn the paper over.

2. Fold the paper from corner to corner in both directions, then unfold.

3. Use the existing creases to pull the sides of the paper toward the center. Allow the paper to collapse into a triangle.

4. Fold the bottom corners of the top layer to the point. Repeat these folds on the back side of the model.

5. Fold the corners of the top layer to the center. Repeat behind.

6. Fold the tips of the top layer down to the center triangles. Repeat behind.

7. Tuck the two small triangles into the pocket of the center triangles. Repeat behind.

8. Spread the layers of the model apart slightly. Blow gently into the bottom hole to form a cube. Shape the cube's sides with fingers as needed.

9. Carefully insert a bulb from the string of lights into the hole.

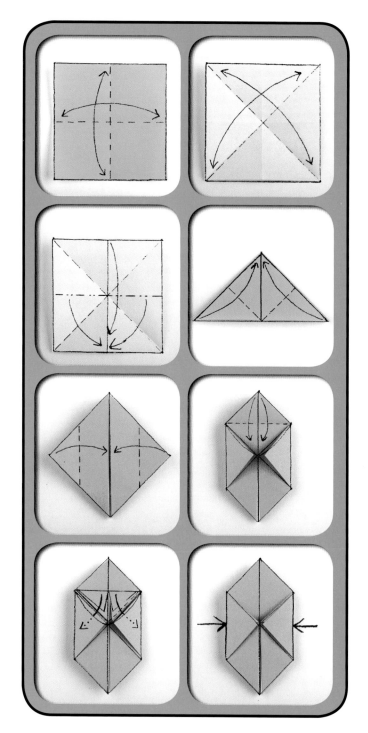

Origami Wisdom: Always press down firmly so that the creases are nice and crisp! Firm folding is a big part of origami success.

Outlook: Good

Today's fortune: "You will make an amazingly easy yet tasty recipe." Find out how to make these beloved crispy cookies.

- small strips of paper
- cookie decorating marker
- hand mixer
- 2 egg whites
- ¼ cup (60 mL) white sugar
- 4 tablespoons (60 mL) butter, melted
- ½ cup (120 mL) flour, sifted
- ¼ teaspoon (1.2 mL) vanilla extract
- baking sheet
- parchment paper

1. Write fun fortunes on small strips of paper with a cookie decorating marker.

2. Use a hand mixer to whip egg whites until they're foamy.

3. Add sugar. Continue to mix until soft peaks form.

4. Add butter, flour, and vanilla. Mix until combined.

5. Drop a tablespoon of batter onto a baking sheet lined with parchment. Use the spoon to spread the batter in an even circle. Bake only a few cookies at a time.

6. Bake at 350°F (180°C) for six to eight minutes.

7. When cookies are golden, remove from the baking sheet with a spatula and place on cool surface. Place a fortune onto each cookie.

8. Work quickly to fold cookie in half over the fortune. Then bend the cookie over the edge of the spatula to form a crescent.

Other Ideas

- To give your cookies a bright burst, color the batter with food coloring before baking. Drop dots of colored batter onto uncolored batter rounds to create patterns.

- Use extracts to make orange, lemon, coconut, or other flavored cookies. Add a 1-ounce (30-gram) square of melted baking chocolate for chocolate cookies.

- Surprise your guests with a shower of color! Add edible pearls, large sprinkles, or confetti before you fold the fortune cookie in half.

- Pipe decorations onto cookies with melted candy coating and a piping bag.

- Dip one half in chocolate and the other half in white chocolate for yin-yang cookies.

- Make giant cookies! Make the dough balls as large as you want. Follow the other instructions. For extra fun, fold mini cookies into the giant one so you have cookies inside cookies.

Find inspiration for fabulous fortunes at
www.perfectpartiesguide.com/downloads

Teeny Umbrellas, Big Fun!

Pint-sized parasols instantly make anyone think they're on vacay! But the kinds sold in stores are everywhere. Make your own—and then turn them into a colorful wreath.

- scalloped circle craft punches (or paper pre-cut in scalloped circle shapes)
- heavyweight paper
- scissors
- toothpicks
- craft or hot glue
- seed beads
- foam wreath form
- plastic lei

1. Use the craft punch to cut out scalloped circles.

2. Cut a line to the center of the circle.

3. Bend and glue the circle into a cone shape. Hold until the glue has set.

4. Poke the toothpick through the center of the cone. Ensure a bit of the pointy end sticks out.

5. Glue the toothpick to the underside of the paper cone. Glue a bead to the top of the toothpick. Hold until the glue has set.

6. Stick the sharp end of the umbrella into the wreath form.

7. Continue working your way around the top and sides of the wreath. Alternate colors and sizes for maximum effect. (Leave the back free so that it can lie flat against the wall.)

8. Use the lei to hang your wreath.

Other Nifty Uses for Paper Umbrellas

- Buy a round white paper lantern and cover the outside of it with umbrellas.

- Use a tiered stand as a cupcake tower and stick a paper umbrella into each cupcake.

- Make mini umbrellas. Do not add toothpicks. Instead, make the mini umbrellas into pendants, earrings, or a lei.

- Brush umbrellas with thinned glue, and sprinkle with glitter. Add a second coat of glue once the first is dry, to reduce glitter shedding.

- Cut out plain circles. Use stamps or smaller hole punches to create decorations in the paper. Or use doilies instead of paper.

- Decorate the paper with strips of washi tape. Let the edges of the tape overlap the paper a little, to create a ruffled effect.

- Leave a slight gap at the top of the paper when forming the cone. Skip the toothpick, and run the umbrella onto a straw instead.

Better With Ranch

Everyone loves ranch dip—but don't your guests deserve better than bottled? Making your own ranch dip couldn't be easier!

- 7 ounce (210 grams) container Greek yogurt
- 1 teaspoon (5 mL) fresh chives
- 1 teaspoon (5 mL) fresh dill
- 1 teaspoon (5 mL) fresh parsley
- 2 cloves garlic, minced
- 1 teaspoon (5 mL) onion powder

- 2 tablespoons (15 mL) olive oil
- squeeze of fresh lemon juice
- salt and pepper, to taste
- French bread
- vegetables, cut into sticks

1. Combine all ingredients in a bowl. Let sit in the refrigerator for at least three hours, or overnight. Keep cold until it's time to serve.

2. Cut French bread into 3-inch (7.6-cm)-long pieces. Then cut each piece at an angle, to create triangles. Make cuts a little off center, so each triangle has a base.

3. Hollow out some of the soft bread, to make a cup.

4. Place a spoonful of ranch dip inside each cup. Add veggies.

Tips: If the bread gets too soggy, lightly toast the cups in an oven before adding the dip.

If you don't have fresh herbs, dry are OK. Use one-third the amount of dried herbs in place of fresh.

Presentation is Key

It may be just veggies and ranch, but that doesn't mean you can't dress it up!

OTHER GREAT IDEAS:

- Going gluten-free? Use hollowed-out zucchini, tomato, cucumber, or bell pepper instead of bread. A corn taco salad shell or an empty lemon rind are good alternatives too.

- Serve veggie cups on a cupcake stand.

- Use mini terra-cotta pots decorated with washi tape instead of bread. Little carrots garnished with fresh parsley are a nice finishing touch.

- Cut long veggies, such as carrots, peppers, celery, and zucchini, into sticks. Skewer softer objects, such as tomatoes, mushrooms, and olives, with toothpicks. Top each toothpick with a tiny pom-pom, or use a paper umbrella.

Feeling Festive

Psst! Want to know the trick to planning a party that truly stands out from the rest? Answer: truly creative thinking. There are a few quick tricks for transforming your party into something totally you-nique.

- Fill balloons with confetti or stars for a glitter-rific effect; you can also buy or make sequined candles for that extra special sparkle. Extra-large balloons also add a major "wow" factor.

- Rather than using a traditional wreath on the door, hang a colorful rainbow tutu! You're sure to get tons of compliments about your style being on pointe.

- Give ordinary food a special twist. Take time to create foods that fit your theme. Think out of the box and try making eats from scratch. Little touches, such as garnishes, favors, or servingware, really help your party stand out.

- Go big or go home! Get creative with cookie cutters, washi tape, food coloring, paper crafts, and printables. These simple and inexpensive items can really amp up your party theme.

- Go out of your way to let guests know you're thinking about them. Make sure anyone on a special diet will get enough to eat. Avoid anything that might cause an allergic reaction, such as nut products or latex balloons. Tailor favors to suit each guest's favorite colors or styles.

Earn Your Stripes

You've learned how to make layered drinks and colored ice cubes. Now combine the two to make a striped cube! Choose juices of different shades and lemonades that would go well together taste-wise. Create the layers by filling ice cube trays about one-third of the way full. Freeze completely. Repeat with two other liquids until the tray is full. Serve in sparkling water.

P-A-R-T-Y!

What time is it? Party time, but of course! (Cue confetti and noisemakers.) It's a big "yay" moment. You've spent weeks planning and priming your place for the big bash – and it's finally time to see it come to life. Get the lowdown on how to lead the party with grace and style. You'll also find out the real deal on handling everything from party crashers to ever-present parents. It all comes back to the key to being a great hostess – putting fun first and going with the flow!

 Find more party tips at
www.perfectpartiesguide.com/tips

Par-tay! (It's Finally Time)

The clock is ticking. In just a short time, your guests will be walking through that front door. Will you be ready? Use this checklist to keep your day-of-party prep on track.

☐ Eat something. A hostess running on empty is a recipe for disaster! Eat foods that will fill you up now and give you energy for later. Fruits and veggies are always good choices. Add a handful of pumpkin seeds and a square or two of dark chocolate, and you'll be fueled up by party time.

☐ Do a final clean sweep a few hours before the party begins. Clear any clutter, dust or wipe down any surfaces that need it, and give rooms one final vacuum.

☐ You've probably completed most of the cooking over the last few days. Now is the time to finish prepping and presenting your food! Ask your parents to help you complete any kitchen tasks that still need to happen before guests arrive.

☐ If need be, make a quick run to the store for any emergency needs or things you may have forgotten. Even better—send a family member with a list. That will give you more time to prep.

☐ All of your hard work is about to get the spotlight. If you haven't already, set up any last-minute decorations.

De-Stress R/x

Just hours away from the party, you're feeling anything but calm, cool, and collected. Sound familiar? You're not alone—lots of party planners feel frazzled right before things get going. Avoid having a hostess meltdown by following a few simple rules.

Beat the rush. If you think party prep will take three hours, make it four! Prep work always takes longer than expected, and starting early will guarantee plenty of time to deal with any pesky last-minute probs.

Pump up the volume. Get into the party spirit before guests arrive by turning on some tunes! Listening to music as you get ready will make it more fun and melt away the stress.

Phone a friend. Why do everything solo when you can harness the power of two? It's practically in the BFF contract that your bestie will be there to help you when you need it. Enlist a friend to come early and help you and your family whip everything into shape.

Leave time for looking great. Lots of hostesses get stuck rushing around and end up barely dressed when the party starts. Don't be that girl! When figuring out your prep time, work in an hour for getting pretty. Take time for a relaxing shower and to primp properly. This extra time will help you look good—and feel great—in your party outfit by the time the guests arrive.

Get the Party Started

If your party is starting off with a whimper rather than a bang, no need to call party 9-1-1. Sometimes all you need is a quick kickstart! Icebreaker games are an easy way to melt any tension and to put everyone at ease. Say "so long" to awkward moments with these awesome ideas:

Play The Name Game

Learning everyone's name can sometimes be a tall task. So why not make it more memorable? In this game, each person introduces herself by turning each letter of her name into a silly acronym. The more out-there, the better! Some examples:

Britt = Britt ran into the tater tot
Ashley = Ashley slurps hot lava each year

Share or Dare

Learn more about your guests with a guessing game! Using small sheets of paper, write up a bunch of "shares" and "dares" designed to learn more about your guests. For example, a share could be: "What food completely grosses you out?" A dare could be: "Imitate your fave celeb and have us guess who it is." Place the papers inside colored balloons (using one color for shares and another for dares.) Guests can take turns popping them and playing along!

Fast Track to Fun

Other quickies that are sure to boost the fun factor:

Place game question cards at different points around the party area, inviting your guests to ask each other questions!

Give each guest a bracelet in a single color. Get your guests to trade beads with each other. At the end of the night, each girl should have a rainbow bracelet to take home. Make it a contest, and give a prize to the person with the most colorful bracelet.

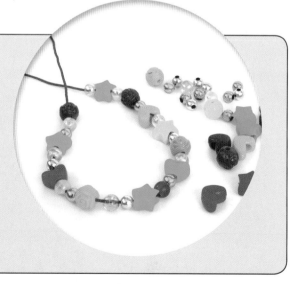

The Usual Suspects

Most people fall into a party personality category. Meet the "usual suspects." Learn how to take on the party peeps who pose a special challenge for the hostess with the mostest.

"THE COMPLAINER":

Nothing is ever quite good enough for this hard-to-please friend. The food is too cold. The music is too loud. The games aren't to her liking. She'll be sure to point out the problem to anyone who cares to listen.

HOW TO DEAL:

Some things are simply out of your control. Explain to the complainer that you're all there to have fun. Why let a little rain or a burnt pizza stop your good time? Your bright attitude just might be contagious.

"THE CHATTY KATHY":

Good old Kathy. She loves to talk and never stops. Once she has your ear, it's hard for her to let go!

HOW TO DEAL:

Put the brakes on this runaway train by putting on your hostess hat. Excusing yourself to refresh the beverages or help out in the kitchen is a subtle yet effective way to escape.

"THE WALLFLOWER":

The party is in full swing, but one of your guests looks like she'd rather be anywhere else. If you spot someone keeping to herself and not joining in, she just might be a wallflower.

HOW TO DEAL:

Not everyone wants to be the life of the party. As the hostess, it's your job to help everyone feel at ease. Make an effort to include the wallflower in your conversation, and steer it toward something you know she likes. Watch her light up when she talks about it.

 Have a question about guests? Ask Mizz Manners at MizzManners.perfectpartiesguide.com

Hostess with the Mostest: Do's & Don'ts

Rolling out the welcome mat for your guests means going the extra mile to meet their needs. Here are some small things you can do that will make a big difference!

Do work ahead of time—whether that means setting the tables the day before or putting party favors in bags throughout the week. Getting as much prep work as possible done early will help you feel less frazzled the day of your big 'do!

Don't skimp on food and drink. Running out of these necessities can be a major prob! For a three-hour party, experts suggest having enough beverages for about three drinks per person. For appetizers, figure that each person might eat four to six bites per hour.

Do your best to make everyone feel welcome. Make sure you get to talk to each guest personally at some point during the party. And don't let them sneak out without saying good-bye!

Don't let your guests go hungry! At the beginning of the party, set out small bowls of party mix and other easy nibbles to tide people over until the food is ready. Nothing makes a party go downhill faster than hungry guests.

Do stay relaxed and have a blast. Some hostesses get so busy that they forget to have fun! Put that at the top of your priority list, and you'll be good to go.

Parties are the perfect place for all the people in your life to intersect. If you've invited different groups—school, sports, neighbors—make sure to introduce everyone. Try to find things your guests have in common to help them mingle. If you see someone not talking to anyone, put in special effort to make him or her feel at ease.

Take a read on your guests' mood and energy and be willing to be flexible. The perfect party you planned in your head might not be the one that's best for your guests. If they're not feeling a game or activity, just move on to something different. It's all about going with the flow!

Little Things Mean a Lot

Make a "just in case" basket in the bathroom. Include dental floss, lotion, lip balm, hairspray, and other personal items guests may need.

Ask Mizz Manners for more tips on making your guests feel welcome at MizzManners.perfectpartiesguide.com

Dealing with Disaster! Party Crises 411

Even the best-laid plans can go awry. So what do you do if your party train goes off the tracks? Get a handle on common hostess emergencies:

Bash Crash

Party crasher alert! Every once in a while, a friend might bring someone unexpected, such as a sibling or someone you don't know. Or maybe a few of your siblings decided to make a surprise "appearance." What's a hostess to do?

In most cases, take it in stride by being prepared. Prepare a bit more food and drink than necessary. Make a few extra gift bags, just in case! However, discreetly make sure your parents are cool with the inflated head count.

Super Spill

Even the most careful snacker spills sometimes. Keep some everyday cleaning materials on hand just in case:

- For condiment and drink stains, remove as much of the spill as possible. Then dab the stain with dishwashing liquid. Rinse with white vinegar and cold water.

- For lipstick or other makeup stains, try to remove as much as you can first. Then dab with liquid detergent. Let sit for a few minutes, then rinse.

- For oil or grease, sprinkle with corn starch, baking soda, or baby powder. Let sit for 10 to 15 minutes, then brush off and rinse with cool water.

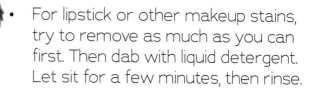

Food Crisis!

A guest with special (and surprising) meal requirements has shown up. Maybe they're trying the latest fad. Or maybe they truly can't eat what's been served. It's up to you to make them feel at home. Ask them questions about what they can and can't eat. Even if you can't come up with anything, they'll appreciate that you tried.

Just a Minute!

The phone just rang. Some of your guests are going to be late. But other guests are already here! Don't sweat it. Start the party as planned. Be sure to make your late guests feel equally as welcome once they arrive!

Recipe Disaster!

One of your recipes didn't turn out. Now what? If you've got plenty of other food, just wipe your mistake off the menu. If you've botched a main dish, make up for it with extra apps or a spare dessert. If you really can't cover, ask your parents if it's OK to get something delivered.

Murphy's Law: Something Will Go Wrong

Remember that fun is the name of the game! If your homemade cookies crumble or you can't find your special party shoes, take a deep breath and move on. If you let one thing ruin your whole day, that will be how you remember your party. Let it go and live it up!

Keep the Party Poppin'

Momentum is a big part of any party. It's important not to let it burn out too soon! Part of a hostess' job is to sustain the shindig and make sure guests have a great time right up until closing time. Luckily, there are a few secret tricks of the trade.

Plan your party layout ahead of time. Do you want use different rooms for different parts of the party? Keep everyone outside? Think about the flow of activities and how you want to spend the day, and use that to decide where to place the different party elements. Proper spacing is key. It's important to make sure people aren't too spread out or all crowding into one small area.

Don't be afraid to delegate! Enlist one of your more outgoing friends as a secret helper. She can help you keep the energy level up and the conversation lively. She can also keep an eye out for people who might need a social pick-me-up. Ask another friend if they'll play "waiter." Having someone else worry about dirty dishes will be one less thing on your plate.

Choose your party times carefully. If it starts too early or ends too late, your guests may decide to show up later or leave early. And consider how long you want your party to be. Two to three hours is a good starting point. If you want your guests to stick around longer, plan things to fill the time. Movie nights or sleepovers are great ways to keep the party going into the wee hours.

Unless photo ops are part of your party theme, ask people to turn off their phones. Keep them focused on what's happening right now.

Introduce your guests as they arrive. Get the conversation flowing right away to help guests mingle. Try some of these icebreakers to keep guests chatting.

If your life was a TV show, which one would it be? Sitcom or drama?

If someone's underwear was showing, would you say something?

Would you rather be super smart or super popular?

If your life had a theme song, what would it be?

Would you rather be the worst player on the best team, or the best player on the worst team?

Would you rather time travel to the past or the future?

If you could invite any three people over for dinner, who would you ask?

If you could be any famous person, who would you be?

Putting the "Super" in Supervision

Having parents around doesn't equal no fun. Though it may seem somewhat uncool to have adults hanging around, trust that you'll be grateful they were there. To help supervision go as smoothly as possible, study strategies for success.

- [ ] Review plans for the party together the day before.

- [ ] Agree on a plan for what to do if uninvited guests find their way in.

- [ ] Go over the ground rules, such as leaving the lights on and keeping certain rooms off-limits. Be sure to discuss what will happen if someone breaks a rule.

- [ ] Agree on when your parents will be present and when they'll let you and your friends do your own thing.

- [ ] What will happen if there's an emergency? Having a plan in place will help for those just-in-case moments.

- [ ] Divvy up the workload and decide who will do what. Some parents find that serving food and drink throughout the party helps them be present without hovering.

- [ ] Don't forget about the parents of your guests. Get familiar with their rules before the party begins. If a guest's parents aren't OK with her wearing nail polish, make sure you have something else for her to do at your spa party.

- [ ] Remember, it's their house too. Be willing to make compromises about who will be where and when.

It's all about figuring out a system that works for you and your family. You'll be glad you did!

Don't forget to thank your parents after the party is over. You don't have to send them a thank-you note, but be sure to let them know you had a great time!

It's Over! Now What?

The party's over! Wishing you could fast forward to the part where the house is clean again? Though you can't wave a magic wand, there are plenty of ways to get your space spic-and-span in a snap.

- [ ] Form a cleanup crew. See if you can bribe your sibs or a few friends to stay afterward and keep the party going. You can entertain yourselves by dishing the "dirt" from the party.

- [ ] Check for any carpet or furniture stains. If you happen to find one, soak it up with a paper towel, then apply stain remover according to the directions (or your parents!)

- [ ] Do a clean sweep of the party area. Use two trash bags to separate actual trash and recyclable items.

- [ ] Place all usable leftover food in containers, and dispose of the rest. Keep in mind how long each food item has been at room temperature, and how well it will keep.

- [ ] Load the dishwasher and let it run as you clean. No dishwasher? No problem. Let dishes soak in the sink as you clean.

- [ ] For an indoor party, vacuum and/or mop floors in the areas where your guests hung out.

- [ ] Store any pieces of décor, party favors, or other items you want to save in a large plastic bin. You can also hang a few pieces in your room as a memento of your mega-awesome day.

Tips on Speeding Up the Clean Up Before, During, and After

Start the party with the cleanest possible space. Your house will be back to spic-and-span with just a quick wipe-down after the party.

Use disposable cups, plates, and other servingware to minimize dish washing time. If you're concerned about waste, look into compostable or biodegradable items.

Have plenty of trash cans available during the party. Label any non-trash cans, such as recyclables or compostables. Your guests will clean up after themselves.

Send your guests home with leftovers. You'll spend less time looking for fridge space after the party.

Gracias, Merci, Thank You!

The good news: The party was a smash success. The bad news: It's true that a hostess' job is never done! Even if your party didn't involve gifts, thanking guests just for being there is a classy thing to do. Luckily, the secrets to writing thank-you notes are simple.

Always send within two weeks of the party date. Set time aside after the party for this task so you don't forget. Buy nice stationary, stamps, and a great pen before the party. It won't seem like such a chore if you're looking forward to it!

SPOTLIGHT SPECIFIC DETAILS, SUCH AS A CONVERSATION BETWEEN YOU TWO OR A WAY THEY CONTRIBUTED. PERSONALIZED DETAILS WILL LET YOUR GUESTS KNOW YOU REALLY APPRECIATED THEIR APPEARANCE.

The hostess gift you brought was unexpected, but very appreciated!

I can't believe how good that blue polish looked on you! You really rocked the rock star look.

Thank you so much for coming to my party and bringing that amazing artichoke dip! I can't stop craving it!

We'll definitely have to go get that mani/pedi soon—my treat! Heart ya!

Your outfit was amazing! Maybe we can get together and exchange ideas for the next costume party!

That was so thoughtful of you to make and it really rounded out the menu.

ALWAYS GO HANDWRITTEN! A NOTE WRITTEN ON A COMPUTER CAN LOOK IMPERSONAL. WHIP OUT YOUR FAVORITE PEN AND TAKE AN EXTRA MOMENT TO MAKE YOUR GUESTS FEEL EXTRA SPECIAL.

May 2014

Dear Ella,

Just writing to thank you for coming to my pirate party! I really appreciated your help keeping the rowdier guests in line. Good thing we didn't have to keelhaul anyone!

Feeling marooned without you!

xoxoxo (and another x to mark the spot!)

Allie

September 2014

Dear Jackie,

Thank you so much for coming to my mustache bash! Where did you find that great stick-on 'stache? It rocked! And you are awesome at guessing mustaches. Next time I'm going to put you in charge of the guessing game!

From one 'stash sista to another,

Paige

Find printable thank-you notes to match your party theme at www.perfectpartiesguide.com/downloads/thank-yous

Picture Perfect

Posting photos online after the party is a given. But what about an actual scrapbook that you can keep forever? Creating a physical book allows you to preserve elements like the invitation, printables, and other things that deserve the spotlight way past the party. It also provides a place to store all the awesome photos from party central! Keep the party going by inviting your buds to take a scrapbooking class together. You can relive the party while creating something great.

Gather all of your pix in a scrapbook, along with any other event mementos. Every time you look through it, you'll remember your picture-perfect party!

As for playing photographer, don't forget to take pictures during your party. (You can also place disposable cameras around the house for people to help you out!) For best results, snap a diverse collection of shots:

DETAIL SHOTS OF YOUR FOOD, SIGNATURE SIPS, GAMES, AND DÉCOR

RANDOM, UNPOSED CANDIDS THAT TELL THE REAL STORY OF THE PARTY

PICTURE OF THE WHOLE GROUP (ONE POSED AND ONE "WILD")

POSED PICTURES OF YOU AND YOUR FRIENDS

Upload your party pics to
www.perfectpartiesguide.com/photos
for a chance to be featured on our blog!

The Fun Never Ends

From planning to prep to party time, you've been on a pretty fantastic voyage! Congrats on a job well done—you've made the grade and earned an "A" in the art of being a hostess. Your next mission, should you choose to accept it? Pick a different theme and do it all over again! And take a deep breath: this book is here to show you the way.

PARTY PREP IN REVIEW

Choose a date!
Set time, place, budget, guest list, menu, party theme, and other important details.

Invite people!
Choose a guest list and send out invites.

Talk it over!
Discuss ground rules and supervision with parents or guardians. Have a plan in place for "what ifs."

Plan ahead!
Plan shopping lists and menus, favors, games, activities, and other party aspects. Practice recipes ahead of time and think about how they will be served and stored.

Clean, clean, clean!
Do a before and after cleaning of your party space. It's always nice to leave a space neater than the way you found it!

Viva la Celebration!

☐ **Make it yours!**
Customize decorations and other party pieces to fit your style and theme. Have fun with favors, food, and beverages to turn any party into your party.

☐ **Engage your guests!**
Your guests are there to have a good time. Make sure everyone is eating, drinking, and being merry!

☐ **Have a great time!**
Take a moment to relax and enjoy yourself! Taste the food, talk to your friends, and don't sweat the small stuff.

☐ **Tie up any loose strings.**
Clean up, send out thank-yous, and start planning for the next perfect party!

 For more party ideas, downloadables, and tips, visit www.perfectpartiesguide.com

Jen Jones Donatelli is a Los Angeles-based author who has written many books for Capstone, including *10 Things You Need to Know About Throwing Parties*. When she's not pinning cute party ideas on Pinterest, Jen also writes about food, lifestyle, and fun for publications including *LA Confidential, San Francisco, Whole Life Times, Thrillist, Shoptopia,* and many more. She is also a graduate and current adjunct faculty member of the E.W. Scripps School of Journalism at Ohio University.

Capstone Young Readers are published by Capstone, 1710 Roe Crest Drive, North Mankato, Minnesota 56003.
www.capstoneyoungreaders.com

Library of Congress Cataloging-in-Publication Data
Jones, Jen.
Planning perfect parties : the girls' guide to fun, fresh, unforgettable events / by Jen Jones.
    pages cm
Summary: "Ideas, inspirations, and tips on how to plan the perfect party"—Provided by publisher.
  ISBN 978-1-62370-063-8 (paperback)
1. Children's parties—Juvenile literature.
2. Parties—Planning—Juvenile literature.
3. Handicraft for girls—Juvenile literature.
4. Girls—Social life and customs—Juvenile literature. I. Title.

GV1205.J648 2014
793.2'1—dc23   2013035803

Printed in China by Nordica.
1013/CA21301920
092013   007745NORDS14

Editor: Mari Bolte
Designer: Tracy Davies McCabe
Photo Stylist: Sarah Schuette
Project Creators: Sarah Schuette and Marcy Morin
Production Specialist: Kathy McColley

Photo Credits:
Key: t=top, l=left, r=right, b=bottom, m=middle, bk=back, fr=front, bg=background.

Photography by Capstone Studio: Karon Dubke except: Dreamstime: Dmitriy Shironosov, 80t; Shutterstock: aboikis, 29b, Adnes Kantaruk, 63rm, Africa Studio, 22, 46lm, alejandro dans neergaard, 112, Alexander Raths, 110, Alexey Stiop, 64t, AlexKol Photography, 72r, Alliance, 12, andreasnikolas, 3lm, Andrew Burgess, 6l, Ariwasabi, 18t, ArtFamily, 54t, Baleika Tamara, 74, Beata Becla, 65m, bestv, 84, BooHoo, 11bm, Brian Goodman, 29bm, chrisbrignell, 58b, chrisbrignell, 80br, Christian Bertrand, 98mr, Coprid, 106, cosma, 73b, DEKANARYAS, 83r, Denisa V, 98ml, DenisNata, 65br, Designs Stock, 82t, dgmata, 62t, Diana Taliun, 98tl, dodi31, 64m, Edyta Pawlowska, 15bk, 71, Elena Dijour, 54m, Elena Elisseeva, 7, Els Jooren, 63lm, ever, 18br, Feng Yu, 18tr, Filip Fuxa, 28b, Firman Wahyudin, 119, Garsya, 24, Gemenacom, 102b, Goran Bogicevic, 21, Gordana Sermek, 63b, haveseen, 82l, Hawk777, 98tr, Iakov Filimonov, 113t, Invisible Studio, 123b, Ipsener, 73t, itman_47, 88b, Ivonne Wierink, 62m, Jackiso, 6r, James Robey, 73r, jcjgphotography, 33t, Jeka, 32b, JMiks, 17fr, Joana Lopes, 109b, Joe Hamilton Photography, 56l, kaarsten, 113b, Käfer photo, 21linset, Kalenik Hanna, 121, Kamenetskiy Konstantin, 109t, kearia, 10r, 123t, Kesu, cover br, 46t, kiboka, 30t, Iakov Filimonov, 105br, LanKS, 63t, Lena Pantiukh, 11tm, lenetstan, 30b, Lidi Papp, 102t, Loredana Cirstea, 18m, Lucky Business, 105t, Lusoimages, 64b, Magdalena Kucova, 52tr, Malivan_luliia, 86b, Mandy Godbehear, 17bk, Marie C Fields, 62b, 65bl, Mariontxa, 23, Matthew Nigel, 72l, mayamaya, 75, Mediagram, 54l, Melanie DeFazio, 33b, Monkey Business Images, 14l, 104t, nikkytok, 80bl, Odua Images, 116, Olivier Le Queinec, 20t, Ozgur Coskun, 65t, Philip Stridh, 29tm, pink pig, 11r, prudkov, 105bl, racom, 108, Rob Marmion, 104b, Robyn Mackenzie, 28m, Ruth Black, 36all, 37all, 39all, 63l, Sarah Cates, 76, Sea Wave, 46rm, senkaya, 18b, sittipong, 10l, Smileus, 82r, Stephen Rees, 28t, Steve Collender, 61t, stockcreations, 27, Susan McKenzie, 49tr, szefei, 54b, Tamara Kulikova, 98b, Tatiana Popova, 28r, 120, Teeratas, 43b, Tenki, 88t, Teresa Kasprzycka, 3r, 29t, 111, Valentina Razumova, 73l, Valua Vitaly, 46b, Shutterstock/Vankad, 9, Vasya Kobelev, 11l, Venus Angel, 32t, violetblue, 104m, VolkOFF-ZS-BP, 42t, Wollertz, 89

Design Elements:
Design Elements and backgrounds by Capstone Studio: Karon Dubke except: Shutterstock:, andersphoto, Andrei Zarubaika, Andrey_Kuzmin, Cecilia Lim H M, EV-DA, Jack Jelly, Lasse Kristensen, Liv friis-larsen, More Images, nikkytok, NUMAX3D, Petrosg, quinky, qvist, SoleilC, VectorForever, Yganko, yienkeat, zsooofija